GOD'S MESSAGE

GOD'S MESSAGE

*A Book of
366 Daily Meditations*

by
366 Christian Leaders
from the
United States,
Canada, and Great Britain

ZONDERVAN PUBLISHING HOUSE
A Division of the Zondervan Corporation
Grand Rapids, Michigan

"The Lord gave the word; great was the company of those that published it."

Psalm 68:11

FOREWORD

In this collection of crisply and sensitively written daily devotionals the reader will discover a deep awareness of basic Bible truths expressed in meaningful and unusually penetrating fashion. The contributors have written out of hearts moved with gratitude for God's goodness and fired with enthusiasm for the cause of Christ. And this spirit of gratitude and enthusiasm is everywhere apparent in the daily meditations even though they come from men in many different denominations and out of various theological traditions.

It is the fervent hope of the publishers that this thoughtful book will continue to have a broad ministry among God's people the world over.

THE PUBLISHERS

G OD'S MESSAGE is the growth of an inspiration that found its origin in the wonderful service that God's Minute has been accomplishing. Hardly a day passes that we do not hear from someone that cherishes this little classic of daily prayers.

God's Minute has proved such a Spiritual help, has brought so much solace and comfort, and it has greatly encouraged religious devotion in the home.

With the eager co-operation of the eminent Clergymen of various denominations of the English speaking world who contributed these little messages in the form of meditations, sermonettes or personal experiences, we offer God's Message to the public with the earnest desire that it will carry on the splendid work of its predecessor.

May the blessings of God be showered upon every reverent reader of this little volume.

IT is not much to give God a minute, but in these so called busy times a minute is better than no time at all.

May these Messages incite to longer periods of devotional thought.

SINCERE thanks and grateful appreciation are hereby extended to all contributors whose co-operation made this little volume possible.

It is our sincere regret that we could not include all of the messages so graciously sent.

GOD'S MESSAGE

LIST OF CONTRIBUTORS

vii

"God—hath shined in our hearts, to give the light of the knowledge of the glory of God in the face of Jesus Christ."—2 Corinthians 4: 6.

HOW shall we gain a knowledge of God? Through a book? Through nature?

God reveals Himself in a Person—"in the face of Jesus Christ!"—the "image of the invisible God." When we know God, then His words and works bear witness to Him, the heavens declare His glory, and nature is filled with spirit; we believe the New Testament because it is the revelation of One who is to us "the Way, the Truth, and the Life."

The greatest thing in the world is to know God as revealed in the life of His Son. The noblest life is to live as His children that we may reveal to others the blessings of His Presence, His Guidance, and His Peace.

THOMAS J. GARLAND, D.D., LL.D., D.C.L.,
Bishop of Pennsylvania.

"He maketh me to lie down in green pastures."—Psalm 23: 2.

THIS nightingale Psalm, which sets the heart singing, is a sparkling gem. Many a morning David led his sheep into green pastures, and caused them to lie down by letting them eat until satisfied. He pondered over the Great Shepherd satisfying us with spiritual blessings that we too, would lie down in green pastures.

Where are the Lord's pastures? In Psalm twenty-two is a picture of Calvary and the Lord crying "My God, My God, why hast thou forsaken me?" In Psalm twenty-four is a picture of heaven with its song, "Lift up your heads, oh ye gates." So you see the "green pasture" Psalm is right in between. Christian, think of it! You dwell in a place bounded on one side by Calvary, which breaks the storms that would sweep over you; and on the other by heaven, the sunny side toward which you are traveling.

Just gaze at your situation. Beauties are there which you never thought of. You live in a spiritual oasis. Yes indeed, "He maketh me to lie down in green pastures."

REV. ROSS H. STOVER, D.D.,
Philadelphia, Pennsylvania.

"I have called thee by thy name; thou art mine."—Isaiah 43: 1.

THERE is no reason in this life for apology, timidity, misgiving. Each one of us has been born for a purpose. Every one is a personality. No man is a worm of the dust. It is not right to cringe. To crawl is unworthy. The supremacy of personality is the burden of the teaching of Jesus. The gospel lifts the individual from obscurity. All through the Bible the individual soul is exalted above system.

Statistics should not overwhelm the spirit. Crowds do not determine one's destiny. Machines are the least permanent of the human order. You are lost in the big city. You are adrift in the small village. The fact is you are never lost. You are never adrift if you choose to believe in your own supremacy. To believe in your own unconquerable soul is not egotism but sense. God says, "I have called thee by name, thou art mine."

REV. WILLIAM EWART DUDLEY, D.D., *Brooklyn, New York.*

"Be thou faithful unto death, and I will give thee a crown of life."—Revelations 2 : 10.

SEMPER FIDELIS" (Always Faithful). This motto of the United States Marine Corps, that organization of valiant soldiers of the sea who have never known retreat. It is a splendid motto for the Christian. Loyalty is the great essential of life. "There may be mistaken loyalties but loyalty itself is never mistaken." The history of Christianity contains the record of lives of untold millions who heeded the exhortation of this challenging text.

On April 21, 1873, Livingstone wrote in his Journal in a shaky hand, "Tried to ride, but was forced to lie down, and they carried me to the village exhausted." On the morning of May 4th his servant found him, not in bed, but kneeling at the bedside with his head buried in his hands upon the pillow. He had died in the act of prayer. Alone, in the heart of Africa, he left his tired worn body for the eternal home.

"O God, to us may grace be given
To follow in their train."

REV. DANIEL STEVENS,
San Francisco, California.

"My grace is sufficient for thee."—2 Corinthians 12:9.

HAVE you ever felt within your own self a something resisting you, checking your development, making partially impotent your most consecrated efforts? And then, no doubt, you did what others have done: you prayed that the weakness, the limiting condition, might be removed. But was it? Certainly not always. Like St. Paul's thorn in the flesh, it remained to thwart you, to defeat your purposes, to frustrate your work. That has been our experience a hundred times. When the thorn is not taken away, what shall we do? Despair, and make our lives more impotent still? No! Rather listen for the divine assurance, "My grace is sufficient for thee." Over us, in our weakness and even in our sin, is a gracious God, loving us with an unmerited love. Would we want—could we ask more?

REV. PAUL J. HOH,
Chestnut Hill, Pennsylvania

"Whatsoever thy hand findeth to do, do it with thy might."——Ecclesiastes 9 : 10.

DURING the construction of our new church building, my attention was frequently attracted to the painstaking care displayed by one of the colored laborers. He always seemed ready with pick and shovel, rake and broom to clear away the rubbish and débris left by others. Only occasionally I saw him with a chisel and a hammer and then only to destroy what failed to pass the inspection of the architect or the committee. In a teasing mood I approached him upon such an occasion and said, "Lee, why must you always destroy? Why don't they sometimes let you build?" His answer indicated a deep philosophic insight into life for he replied, "Boss, I knows my place!" Oh, that we would always recognize our place and be ready to destroy if need be so that others might build anew, willing to give the credit unto others.

REV. CARL AUGUST VOSS, D.D.,
Pittsburgh, Pennsylvania.

"Give for alms those things which are within."—
Luke 11: 41, Revised Version.

SUCH things as ye have," reads the King James version. The Revised Version has it, "Those things which are within." And that does not refer to the things that are within the pocketbook, though the use of the word alms would seem to suggest as much. Many gifts in the long run are worth far more than money. The latter may give temporary relief but when the money is exhausted the need returns.

When Adelina Patti, the great singer, took a little street beggar into her home and taught her to use her voice correctly she did infinitely more for her than if she had filled her begging cup to the brim with gold. Can we not believe that the Master is perhaps thinking of love and brotherliness and kindness and encouragement—these things that are within the heart and in the power of all to give?

REV. WILLIAM S. ABERNETHY,
Washington, D. C.

"As the hart panteth after the water brooks, so panteth my soul after Thee, O God. My soul thirsteth for God, for the living God."—Psalm 42: 1–2.

GOD showers upon us the riches of His never failing bountiful goodness. His mercies are new every morning, every noonday, every evening.

But He has taught us by the experiences of life, that He Himself is the one all-inclusive blessing sufficient for our every need. He gave Himself once to men in the gift of His Son and through Him and by His Holy Spirit He is ever renewing the gift of Himself to all who will receive Him.

This is the blessing for which we thirst—the blessing far exceeding every other gift. If we can but lay hold of this gift then there will be no restlessness, no darkness, no weakness, no sorrow, no deadness, for who hath God wanteth nothing.

Give us Thou Gracious Father both the will and the power to receive Thyself and abide with us and in us through all of time and eternity.

RT. REV. WILLIAM F. ANDERSON, LITT.D., LL.D.,
Boston, Massachusetts.

"The Lord shall PRESERVE thy going out, and thy coming in, from this time forth, and even for evermore."
—Psalm 121: 8.

WE DO not want so much to bring God's approval and blessing down to our plan as to adjust our plans and works to His perfect will. Prayer is not only a receiving, but a seeking and finding His direction and illumination. Let us, like Jotham, prepare all our ways before Him and go forth with the inspiring consciousness that the things we ask are given because He has asked them in us and wants them for us. Let us cover all the coming year with a canopy of His covenant promise and overshadowing presence, and so shall we be "different from all other people of the earth" because "He goeth with us." Thus shall our lives be divinely insured and the Lord shall bless our "going out" and our "coming in, from this time forth, and even for evermore."

REV. WALTER E. EDMONDS,
Glendale, California.

"Having loved . . . He loved unto the end."—John 13 : 1.

LOYALTY needs no definition. At the mention of the word a multitude of relationships run up to say what it is. The community, state, nation, the home, business and others say "we know what it is."

When we connect the words "Jesus" and "Loyalty" we usually think of human loyalty to Him. This tells of a greater loyalty: His loyalty.

He was loyal to us. He might have failed us in the Temptation at Capernaum when they offered Him a crown; at Gadara when He might have made a purely personal following; in Gethsemane and on Calvary. But He was true to our interests.

Our lives ought to reflect His loyalty. We do not meet the day alone, "Lo, I am with you." "He ever liveth to make intercession for us." Stephen saw His interest.

REV. M. JOSEPH TWOMEY, D.D.,
Philadelphia, Pennsylvania.

"In the world ye shall have tribulation: but be of good cheer: I have overcome the world."—John 16: 33.

THIS is not a call to stoicism; nor an urge not to acknowledge defeat however sorely pressed.

It is a solicitation to trust; a proffer of Christ's own unique achievement to those beset by trials too great for their own strength; an invitation to accept the reinforcements we need to glorious victory. Here is a conflict where the victory is not to the strong, but to the believing. "This is the victory which overcometh the world, even your faith." It is the recognition that not all the beautiful and fragrant flowers grow under fair and temperate skies, and in broad fields.

In crannied wall, and under winter snows, too, fair flowers bloom.

REV. WALTER EVERETT SMITH, D.D.,
Wilmington, Delaware.

"Fear thou not; for I am with thee: be not dismayed; for I am thy God: I will strengthen thee; yea, I will help thee; yea, I will uphold thee with the right hand of my righteousness."—Isaiah 41: 10.

FEAR is in the background of more lives than we imagine. It comes in various forms: about the past, the fear of discovery; about the present, the fear of inability; about the future, the fear of insufficiency and uncertainty. God's word through His prophet came to a people dejected and irresolute. They were not able to believe in and to appropriate His plans for their future through the fear that possessed their hearts.

In spite of all the "pep" talks of "personality" promoters we have unavoidable ground for fear when our own strength is our only guarantee. We overlook that which makes the whole difference. "I am with thee." God's guidance and strength and grace are for every soul who will depend on Him and give Him control. In Christ we realize the fulfillment of His promises. (Study Christ's personal promises). "The right hand of God's righteousness" is the seal of this message.

REV. W. T. HALLAM, M.A., D.D.,
W. Hamilton, Ontario, Canada.

''All things work together for good.''—Romans 8: 28.

ALL things! It is as truly of the mercy of God that good fortune shall not harm us as that disaster and sorrow shall not disturb us. The grace of God is as much needed in green pastures as in the desert; as much by the still waters as by the stormy seas.

By this same goodness of God we trust that all the hard and bitter things of life may somehow ripen into sweetness. So if you have a cross, wear it! Wear it proudly and gladly! For any experience, any test or trial, any sorrow or loss, may be so accepted and used, so altered or adapted, so changed or completed, that by it and through it, our lives may be made richer and better.

Rev. J. Percival Huget, D.D,
Brooklyn, New York.

"He endured, as seeing him who is invisible."—Hebrews 11: 27.

WHAT calm, comfort and strength for life these words suggest. To see God in history will smite pessimism with a death blow. To study God's chronology is to find unfailing inspiration for faith. Stephen said: "At that time Moses was born." The Son of Man came "in the fullness of time."

To see God above all secondary causes tranquilizes life. Jacob saw the ladder with the Angels, as secondary causes, moving up and down the ladder, but above it God was watching. The record is that "it came to pass when God would take Elijah up into Heaven." No matter what the nature or causes were that took him—God's will was in it all.

Blessed are the clear-visioned for they see God in all history and in all human affairs. We are not an orphan universe. There is a Father's heart at the center of this universe in which we live and move.

REV. JOHN THOMPSON, D.D.,
Chicago, Illinois.

"Caught up into paradise, and heard unspeakable words."—2 Corinthians 12:4.

WHAT glorious visions were vouchsafed to the Apostle Paul! Caught up into Paradise, and heard unspeakable words. Vision of heaven with its joys, pleasures, and blessings!

In the quiet hour of devotion, we sense especially the nearness of heaven. We are in Paradise. Ours is a distinguished honor to speak with God, a blessed privilege to commune with Him, to hear His words of counsel and guidance, so that "our hearts burn within us" as He talks with us. Thus we are fitted more properly to go forth to our daily tasks, after we have been on the mountain top with God. Thus comforted and strengthened, we are prepared to comfort and strengthen others.

> "To comfort and to bless,—
> To find a balm for woe,—
> To tend the lone and fatherless,—
> Is angels' work below."

REV. J. S. ALBERT,
Indianapolis, Indiana.

"I heard a voice. . . . I was not disobedient. . . . Having therefore obtained help of God, I continue unto this day, witnessing."—Acts 26: 14, 19, 22.

SIMPLE decisions make mighty men. A Vision lures—a Voice calls! To follow means agonizing toil—and greatness! "Whosoever will be greatest among you let him be your servant." Service is one measure of greatness but it must hear a Voice to make it vital.

To many Paul was a mystery. The things that once he had counted gain—in his pre-Christian days—he abandoned completely later. In their place had been set up the love of the Galilean—rejected of men but risen in glory and power. Comforts, friendships, honors, prospects—all were cast aside that he might follow closely in the footsteps of the Crucified.

The great life had heard its Voice summoning to toil and conflict; it had answered, "Ready, Aye, Ready," and in the strength of the Master it had continued witnessing. So it is always—a Voice—Obedience—and by God's help, continued witnessing.

REV. LEWIS FULMER KIPP, B.A.,
Toronto, Ontario, Canada.

"He that loveth not, knoweth not God; for God is love."—1 John 4:8.

LOVE has its origin in God and every person who loves is beginning to know God. That person who is destitute of love has never had any knowledge of God. Jesus came to reveal a God of love. He believed that love was the greatest thing in the world. He not only believed it, but He lived it.

The greatest thing the world has ever discovered about God, is that He is love. To make that discovery is to be saved. Redemption is not a theological dogma. All that God does is an expression of his abiding love; it is changeless. Human hate and sin cannot kill it. A soul cannot drift so far as to be outside the zone of the love of God. The love of God is the hope of the world. Knowing that God loves me, I never need to give up; He will never leave me nor forsake me.

REV. HOWARD G. HAGEMAN,
Albany, New York.

"Prove all things; hold fast that which is good."—1 Thessalonians 5: 21.

NOTHING means more to us than the truths we have proved by our own experience. The young man whose sight has been restored cries: "One thing I know; whereas I was blind, now I see." The anxious father, hopeful and even confident for his demoniacal son, fairly shouts forth: "Lord, I believe; help thou mine unbelief!" And a host of folk down through the years give their vote of confidence to a religious experience whose validity has been proved over and over again by the great test of life itself. These bear a steadfast witness to an experience proved and retained.

They all held fast. Dare we do less if we, too, would live as they lived? Fearless to ask, confident in proof, firm to the end, holding that which has withstood the test, strengthened by power from above, we would also join the great throng and blend our voices in everlasting praise of the Eternal Master of the Ages.

REV. A. MARLAND SHOEMAKER,
Analomink, Pennsylvania

"He that showeth mercy, with cheerfulness."—Romans 12: 8.

THE Apostle Paul is here pointing out the practical duty of showing mercy and he is urging us to do it with cheerfulness. Every day we have numerous opportunities for showing mercy to our fellow men. It may be the simple matter of visiting the sick. It may be that of forgiving someone who has wronged us. But whenever we do have an opportunity to show mercy let us do it with cheerfulness not with a grudging spirit or a long face. The word literally means hilarity. The idea being that we should find great joy in showing mercy. Christ was continually showing mercy. He was always going about doing good and always cheerfully. Let us follow His example. Let us do our daily deeds of mercy with a smiling face and with a singing heart.

REV. GEORGE E. NEWELL,
Wichita, Kansas.

"I will put my law in their inward parts, and write it in their hearts; and will be their God, and they shall be my people."—Jeremiah 31: 33.

THE penalty that we pay for a complicated civilization is in the increase of laws for the regulation and control of ordered life.

It is with life as it is with traffic on our streets, the more conjested it becomes, the more regulations and ordinances have to be enforced.

Our hope for the safety of life and the redemption of society is not in an increase of external law, but in an under-girding of the capacity of men to govern themselves.

Jeremiah saw that it was only by a life of disciplined moral freedom on the inside that salvation could be achieved. He has God say: "I will put my law in their inward parts, and write it in their hearts; and will be their God, and they shall be my people."

REV. OSCAR THOMAS OLSON,
Baltimore, Maryland.

"I will never leave thee, nor forsake thee.—Hebrews 13: 5.

EVERY day we live in God, moves from the evening to the morning, from darkness to the light. He helps us meet our dark problems with radiant faces. If we are facing a temptation that is too much to resist, He is our Shield. If the burden of some one else's sin presses upon the heart, He helps to bear it. If we are living in loneliness because the life that has been our precious companionship has gone from our side, He is a Companion "that sticketh closer than a brother." If we are called to walk through the difficult places, we have One who has journeyed that way and will guard us from stumbling and sustain us by His grace.

REV. ALONZO J. TURKLE, D.D.,
Pittsburgh, Pennsylvania.

"They cast four anchors . . . and wished for the day."
—Acts 27: 29.

A SENSE of security and the dawn of hope!
How reassuring and glorious! Four anchors
God, Hope, Duty, Faith. We shall be kept from
drifting if, for us, God is not an absentee God
but a very present help in time of trouble. Hope
is an anchor found close to our God Who is a
God of hope. "Why art thou cast down, O, my
soul? Hope thou in God." Then there is Duty.
The path of duty always leads to glory. Every
call of duty is a call of God. And Faith! Faith
is confidence. Many good people are full of fears.
A conviction that God is, that the best for us all
lies ahead, that Duty always reveals the next step
we must take and that Right must inevitably triumph, because God is God, will allay our fears.
"Though clouds and darkness are round about His
throne, yet righteousness and judgment are the
habitations of His dwelling place."

REV. JOEL HARPER,
Spokane, Washington.

"But God forbid that I should glory, save in the cross of our Lord Jesus Christ."—Galatians 6: 14.

LAST summer we were building a cobble fireplace at our country home. We had planned to use the stones in their natural state but the contractor suggested that we break them open because of their hidden beauty. Every stone held a surprise. One, worn smooth and drab from exposure and erosion, when broken open, revealed a perfect cross of green against a black background. Literally hundreds came to see the most unusual sight. Familiar verses came to mind. "If these hold their peace even the stones would immediately cry out." Again I thought of Christ's words, "I came not to destroy the law but to fulfil it." I thought of how Christ took the old law, worn, despised and irksome and put the cross at the center and gave it a new meaning. Let us apply this truth to life. If the cross of Christ is central in our lives, no matter what changes come, what the blights and abuses of a cruel world, nothing can effect our peace or change the beauty of our character. "God forbid that I should glory save in the cross."

REV. FREDERICK ALLEN, D.D.,
Troy, New York.

"Jesus, thou son of David, have mercy on me."—Luke 18: 38.

JESUS, Lord, have mercy on me!" For centuries upon centuries the litanies of Christendom have been modeled on that plaintive cry. But sometimes the individual gets lost in the crowd when Jesus is passing by.

Have we not all felt the divine impulse in some way or other as Jesus was passing by and making his appeal to our hearts? It may have been in the sermon we heard or the printed Word, in the affliction we bore or the grief we felt, in the heart-throbs of memory or the burning bush of sleepless worry, in the profound satisfaction of high achievement or the hot tears of disappointment, in the broadening horizon of increasing knowledge or the onrush of new inspiration, in the ecstacy of joy or the thrill of art or eloquence, in the fervency of prayer or the delights of Christian fellowship. These were our opportunities to have Jesus open our eyes by faith upon a world of deep enduring life.

REV. ABDEL ROSS WENTZ, PH.D., D.D., *Gettysburg, Pennsylvania.*

"Be still, and know that I am God."—Psalms 46: 10.

IN THE silences I make in the midst of the turmoil of life I have appointments with God. From those silences I come forth with spirit refreshed, and with a renewed sense of power.

In the momentary hushes of the storm that rages in wild fury around the eaves of my cottage on the lake I hear the gentle patter of the rain upon the roof. At the close of day, when the sounds of work or play are hushed, I hear the soft rustlings of the night, the night's "trailing garments."

From the din of the city street I step in through the door of some old gothic church, where the foot-falls sink softly into the carpet of the aisle, where the sunlight comes in through the stained glass windows and pours its azure and gold around me, and the deep-voiced organ gently sings the song of my heart.

It is so I hear a voice in the silences, and become increasingly aware that it is the voice of God.

REV. DANIEL HEITMEYER,
Milwaukee, Wisconsin.

"Wait on the Lord: be of good courage, and he shall strengthen thine heart."—Psalms 27: 14.

LIFE is our supreme adventure. We need courage to live it. Security we can't have. It would ruin us. Safety first is a vicious principle in the field of moral action. "Live dangerously" is a far wiser watchword. Only by so living can we break the despotism of fear. What we want is mastery, not safety. We have it when we know we are stronger than anything that earth can send against us, "for we are pressed on every side—perplexed—pursued—smitten down." The power to endure is the measure of manhood. Courage is conquest. But lasting valor comes from within—it is mental and spiritual, not muscular. The consciousness of having the power of God at our back gives us a fighting front to life. God and a good man is an invincible company. "We are more than conquerors through Him that loved us."

REV. CHESTER B. EMERSON, D.D.,
Detroit, Michigan

"As thy days, so shall thy strength be."—Deuteronomy 33: 25.

THE joy of living may be interrupted by occasional disappointments and reverses, but these experiences need not lead us to chant a perpetual miserere. Strength is given to break the storm and heaving billow, as well as to sail the ship of life on the calm waters of a tranquil sea. God's hand is on the tiller and He will not allow our bark to founder or sink. Instead of pouring forth the dirge of lamentation, we can still echo the songs of courage and hope. Our little plan so dear to our heart, which has apparently failed, has simply been absorbed into some larger and wider plan which God has in view; our little purpose which we supposed was defeated has been taken up into the eternal purpose of His boundless love. With an unfaltering trust in God's wisdom, we can have the courage to keep on, the courage to do and to dare, to think and to plan, to persevere and fulfill.

REV. FREDERICK A. MACMILLEN,
Reading, Pennsylvania.

"In the beginning God created the heaven and the earth."—Genesis 1:1.
"I am the Lord thy God. Thou shalt have no other Gods before me."—Exodus 20:2-3.

IN THE beginning of time God made the heavenly bodies and the earth, put them in their places, started the machinery of the universe and has kept it going ever since. This was all done for man.

Again, God says, "I am the Lord *thy* God." The Most High God gives Himself to insignificant man. His care is constant. Above are the overshadowing wings; underneath are the everlasting arms. His eye is on the sparrow and I know He watches me.

But God knew that man would be tempted to pay homage to his own devices, be led away from God into worldly pleasures and lose his soul. Hence, God warns, "Thou shalt have no other gods before me."

Let me ask myself, "Is God uppermost in my heart? Does He receive the first fruits of my life?" Let us worship the Lord our God and serve Him alone.

REV. MARION G. RICHARD, A.M..
Collingdale, Pennsylvania.

"But when that which is perfect is come, then that which is in part shall be done away."—1 Corinthians 13: 10.

THE faith of man outruns and outreaches his experience. With our limited understanding we seek to penetrate the past, to know the present, and to discern the future. At best we see through a glass darkly. The road into the past is somewhat obscure. Our conception of life is partial. Our knowledge of God is limited. Our vision of the future is incomplete. We are pilgrims traveling toward the light. The path shineth more and more unto the perfect day. It is a far cry from the wooden plough to the tractor, from the candle to electricity, from Newton to Einstein. The partial is passing. Experience is enlarging. Life is becoming.

Our view of life is often obstructed by some fragmentary experience, some partial understanding. Some day, we are confident, the joys, the struggles, yea, the tragedies of life will all fit into the picture—and it will be a perfect picture.

REV. JAMES G. BRAWN,
Laramie, Wyoming.

"What is your life?"—James 4: 14.

HERE is a serious and solemn question. Let us attempt an answer. Your life is a divinely created gift, one sustained by its Creator. Your life is a divinely purchased possession.

Your life is a sacred trust to be wisely invested. Its real value is not its intrinsic value but in its relationships. Nothing is of any real value apart from its relationships whether it be a dollar, a letter of the alphabet, a note of music or a life. Live apart in spirit and in body from everyone else and you are of no value to God, or man, or yourself. Put your life with all its God-given powers in right relationship first with God and then your fellowmen and it becomes a thing not only of infinite value but of infinite satisfaction and joy. Let us say like Wendell Phillips: "O God, I belong to thee. Take what is thine own. I only ask that what is wrong may have no power of temptation and what is right may take no courage to do it."

REV. LEON STEWART, D.D.,
Port Collins, Colorado.

"What shall a man give in exchange for his soul?"—
Mark 8 : 37.

IF BUT once in our lives we had heard the voice
of Truth; if to our eyes had been granted but
a single glimpse of unearthly Beauty; if only one
call had ever come to us, summoning us to pure
loyalty to Right and to deep communion with God
Most High, it would be enough to make us in our
turn ask Christ's triumphant question: What in
all the world could we accept in exchange for a
soul so favored and so predestined? Our divine
and deathless vocation would be manifest in even
one such vision of the Supreme.

But we have had more than one. Day by day
the veil is lifted and we catch glimpses of the
glory that is ours. When we consecrate sorrow
and make pain sublime by courageous trust; when
in love we serve and forgive; when with Jesus we
stand on the threshold of vision we bear witness
that God is and that His eternal life is our inheritance. Rejoice! You have the priceless gift.
You are God's and He is yours.

REV. WILLIAM L. SULLIVAN,
Philadelphia, Pennsylvania.

"Fear thou not; for I am with thee: be not dismayed; for I am thy God: I will strengthen thee; yea, I will help thee; yea, I will uphold thee with the right hand of my righteousness.—Isaiah 41: 10.

MAN by means of certain devices can multiply his power of arm and eye and ear almost beyond calculation. Electricity always was near man, but only recently has he learned how to use it. Even so resources of spiritual and moral strength are available for everybody.

Of course if one denies this, that's the end of it; for divine help becomes matter of actual knowledge and experience only through experiment.

Faith itself is a source of superhuman strength. He who believes is stronger than he who does not believe. The life of the lower animals is limited because they are cut off from our world of faith and hope. A man who lives only the animal life is similarly circumscribed and weakened.

Bold affirmation and effort put our souls in touch with God.

Strength to do comes only through doing.

REV. CLINTON BALTZELL ADAMS,
Philadelphia, Pennsylvania.

"Your sorrow shall be turned into joy . . . And your joy no man taketh from you."—John 16: 20, 22.

L AST September we lost our only child, a radiant girl on the very threshold of life's deepest and best. At first the sorrow was overwhelming, but a transformation has taken place and now we are resting upon assurances that are complete and abiding. We have the joy of knowing that she is beyond the touch of pain, disappointment, failure or any of life's tragedies—she is in God's keeping, and we ask no better thing than that. We do not understand the reason of her passing, but we know that God is wisdom and love and we are content to wait for his explanation. We are sure also that death has no power to take away our deepest treasures. Her character, our associations and precious memories, all that made our life together remain untouched; they are ours forever more. The assurance of reunion with her in the Land beyond the Shadows girds us with strength and bids us be worthy of our solemn trust. Thus, our sorrow floats upon the bosom of deep tides of joy that nothing can stem or lessen. Our comfort is full and complete!

(CANON) ALLAN P. SHATFORD,
Montreal, Quebec, Canada.

"Yea, though I walk through the valley of the shadow of death, I will fear no evil: for thou art with me; thy rod and thy staff they comfort me."—Psalm 23: 4.

"THE valley of the shadow of death" may refer to any dark, dread or awful experience through which the child of God may be called upon to pass—sorrow, affliction, bereavement, poverty, persecution, death.

It is kind of our Great Shepherd that He permits the valley to come in the middle of the Psalm and not at the beginning; after we have been in green pastures of fellowship with Him and are strengthened for conflict. O, the thoughtfulness of God in our behalf.

The valley of the shadow of death is very narrow. We pass through it in single file. No earthly friend can go with us in death. So we note that the personal pronoun is changed from "he" to "thou," from third to second.

But if you have Christ as Savior and Shepherd you can say: "Though I walk through the valley of the shadow of death I will fear no evil for thou art with me; thy rod and thy staff they comfort me."

REV. WILLIAM EVANS, D.D., PH.D., *Los Angeles, California.*

"Hast thou commanded the morning?"—Job 38: 12.

IF YOU do not command the morning, the morning will command you. If you seek no divine energy at the beginning of the day, attempting to go through on your own strength, you are likely to stall before sundown. Dominate the morning. Do not let the morning dominate you. Have your way with it. Baptize it with prayer; stamp it with gratitude; dedicate it to honest work, unselfish service, quiet courtesy. Make sure that, before you sleep, you will have given a hand to someone worse off than yourself. Take time, before the day's work begins, to draw strength from the infinite sources and then—command the morning, strong for its duties, armored against its dangers and its fears. Master the morning. Let not the day make you his slave.

REV. DANIEL RUSSELL, D.D.,
New York, New York.

"Lo, I have set a door before you which no one is able
to shut; for though your strength is small, you have kept
my word, you have not renounced my Name."—Revelation
3:8. Moffatt's Translation.

THE Divine Friend is ever watching to promote our truest welfare. He finds the occa-
sions whenever we heartily assist Him. Then
opportunity is His reward for our fidelity.

On this particular day you may be confronted
by circumstances and problems that bewilder and
baffle you and the path into the future days may
seem a blind alley. But, if, despite anxiety and
fear, you endeavor to pray, to trust, to be loyal
to the highest you know, you may safely believe
that guiding signals will appear, that wise choices,
decisions, plans will be suggested, that a fair opportunity, and perhaps one wholly unexpected,
will greet you:—that a door will swing wide; for
He Who keeps life's precious doors does not fail
when He sees that we are fit to pass through.

REV. HARRY P. DEWEY, D.D.,
Minneapolis, Minnesota.

"To give unto them beauty for ashes, the oil of joy for mourning, the garment of praise for the spirit of heaviness; that they might be called trees of righteousness, the planting of the Lord, that he might be glorified."—Isaiah 61: 3.

THE beautiful fabric of childhood's dreams, the gay, grand aircastles of youth all too often crumble under the relentless heat of noonday, and leave only a heap of gray ashes for all the promises of life's morning. To mourning souls beside such ashheaps God offers beauty for their ashes. He sends a Friend Who will help the discouraged and brokenhearted to rise up and build anew and to build enduringly.

Life's best for a pile of ashes! Here, then, is earth's greatest transaction. New hope, a new goal and power to achieve all for the emberdust of vanished hopes and, withal, a Friend Who will stay with us and see that disaster does not come a second time. Who will not accept this magnificent offer of divine grace? The real start in life is made when, standing beside our smoldering ashheaps, we reach out and grasp the hand of that Friend Whom God has sent and begin life over with Him.

REV. ARTHUR M. BAKER, PH.D.,
Philadelphia, Pennsylvania.

"Be of good cheer."——Matthew 14:27.

WE ARE anxious to be happy, and happiness is more, as we know, the result of things within than of things without. But if we are to be truly happy within, some things in our lives must be gotten rid of. There is sin, for instance— we must find forgiveness if we are to enjoy real happiness; and the only place where forgiveness may be obtained is at the foot of the Cross. There we may hear the words of Jesus: "Be of good cheer, thy sins are forgiven." There is fear, and anxiety—what better thing is there to do when tossed upon the many waters than to look in faith to the Christ Who comes to us with His word of cheer? There is the last great adventure of life— but "be of good cheer"; Christ has overcome the world, and His victory may be yours and mine.

REV. A. W. SCHATTSCHNEIDER, S.T.D.,
Philadelphia, Pennsylvania.

"Trust in the Lord with all thine heart; and lean not unto thine own understanding. In all thy ways acknowledge him, and he shall direct thy paths."—Proverbs 3 : 5, 6.

A S ONE in special need would consult a physician, banker, or trusted friend for light and direction, should not we bring all our plain and puzzling "ways" unto Him, Who is Infinite Wisdom, exercises Fatherly Love and possesses Omnipotent Power? In so doing we but follow our Saviour and Example, Who, to learn His Father's will, spent whole nights in prayer.

What a gilt-edge, love-laden, proof-lined, God-assured promise is here given us! To follow its instructions is sure to blaze for us a safe, happy and successful pathway through all the intricate and perplexing problems which beset life in all its stages and situations, from early youth to ripened age.

REV. PHILIP C. CROLL, D.D.,
Womelsdorf, Pennsylvania.

"By the grace of God, I am what I am."—1 Corinthians 15: 10.

CHARACTER is the determining factor of human life. The purpose of the religion of Jesus Christ is to create, develop, perfect character. Character is what I am in the sight of God, in the inmost recesses of my being; not what I seem to be nor what I would like others to think I am, but what I am in thought and purpose, in work and in deed. Character is the summing up of all I have thought and said and done. How is it to be secured and strengthened? Paul gives the answer: "By the grace of God." Without it we cannot progress God-wards. With it, we can do all things. It may be had by seeking; its effectiveness may be demonstrated by using. "By the grace of God" we may grow into the likeness of Christ, which is the realization of the Christian character.

RT. REV. JOSEPH M. FRANCIS, D.D.,
Indianapolis, Indiana.

"The blood of Jesus Christ his Son cleanseth us from all sin."—1 John 1: 7.

THE ugliest and most destructive thing in all the world is sin. It is with us when we are born and it follows us to the grave. Even the Christian believer, who is born from above, feels its awful power, and cries out in the words of St. Paul, "who shall deliver me from the body of this death?" Here our text comes filling the sorest need of our heart and satisfying the intensest longing of our soul with its precious message of sins fully paid for and fully forgiven. God had said through the prophet, "Though your sins be as scarlet, they shall be as white as snow; though they be red like crimson, they shall be as wool." God's gracious redemption through His Son had not yet taken place. But the Christian can now take courage; for he has the precious assurance that he is now cleansed from all his sins, and can say with St. Paul, "I thank God through Jesus Christ our Lord."

REV. C. H. LITTLE, D.D.,
Waterloo, Ontario, Canada.

"For we are his workmanship, created in Christ Jesus unto good works, which God hath before ordained that we should walk in them."—Ephesians 2: 10.

So THEN God has a plan for me. It is the result of His foreordination. This thought runs through Paul's letters like a vein of gold. We are God's husbandry, God's building, and here God's "creation," in sense of artistry.

So God has a purpose for me; He exerts His power upon me and exercises patience towards me. For what? The production of good works. In the New Testament "good" always means good in the sense of spiritual beauty. Rich clusters with the bloom upon them. For such works God exercises His power and patience on me. I am comforted by this, and yield myself to its gracious ministry. He will achieve His purpose in, for, and through me. In this way I can be something, and being is doing at its best, for without being, doing misses its inner spiritual quality. Being and doing together, constitute my "walk," and to walk with God means that I am going in the same direction, enjoying His companionship, and moving towards the same goal.

REV. WILLIAM A. FREEMANTLE, D.D.,
Philadelphia, Pennsylvania.

"I am come that they might have life, and that they might have it more abundantly."—John 10: 10.

EVERY normal soul wishes to know and live as full a life as it is capable of enjoying. The tragedy of many a life is that it has sought such a life in false ends and evil ways. Many have listened to bad teachers, or to their own fleshly desires. They know only the animal side of life and never attain to life at its best, or in its fullness of power and joy.

All life is a gift from above from God in "whom we live, move and have our being." We shall never have life in all its fullness of conquest and happiness until we turn to our Lord and Master, Jesus Christ and receive from Him that highest, richest, holiest life, which He alone can give. He is not only our Savior from our sin but is the fountain-head of that water of life, which if received by us creates in us a well of living water which is life abundant and eternal.

REV. EDWIN HEYL DELK, D.D.,
Philadelphia, Pennsylvania.

"Can there any good thing come out of Nazareth?"—
John 1: 46.

MUCH came out of Nazareth. Elijah made it
the center of his labors. It was near Nazareth that Jonah had his home, from which he
went out to proclaim the judgment of God against
a wicked civilization. Nazareth at least gave Jesus
a home while Jerusalem gave Him a cross. People
travel from the ends of the earth to feel its haunt-
ing spell. More prayers are said on earth today
by people whose faces are turned toward Nazareth
than any other place on earth. It was out of this
village that a humble peasant girl tramped to
Judea. Because she had no money and Judea had
no heart she fell asleep in a stable, a mere cave
in a hillside, while cattle chewed their cud, and
the dark, dank cave rang with the bleating of
cattle. Yet out of that sleep of that Nazareth
Mother came a little child who has transformed
the hope of the world. Good did come out of
Nazareth. Paul was right: The foolishness of
men is often made to praise God. The stone which
the builders rejected becomes the headstone of
the corner.

REV. JOSEPH R. SIZOO, D.D.,
Washington, D. C.

"Peace I leave with you; my peace I give unto you: not as the world giveth, give I unto you. Let not your heart be troubled, neither let it be afraid."—John 14:27.

IN PLAYING upon a harp, it is said, it requires as much skill to know upon which strings to place the fingers to stop their vibrations as to know which strings to strike to bring out their music. Life is infinitely more musical than a harp and the heart is capable of greater harmonies than all the instruments made by man. What we need so deeply in our lives is the uplift and comfort of peace, and that is to possess a singing soul. We need something to keep our soul in tune and that is to know what to include and what to exclude. Outward trouble and commotions there may be which sweep across our lives but they are powerless to invade that inner sanctuary. Just as the ocean may be wind-swept and storm-tossed, but the waves sink no further below the level than they rise above it, while underneath are the tranquil depths where the myriad life of the ocean goes on. This our peace: . . .

"God's greatness flows round our incompleteness,
Round our restlessness His rest."

RT. REV. CHARLES E. WOODCOCK, D.D., LL.D.,
St. Matthews, Kentucky.

"My sheep hear my voice, and I know them, and they follow me; and I give unto them eternal life; and they shall never perish, neither shall any man pluck them out of my hand."—John 10: 27, 28.

HERE is a passage that has brought, in times of trial, perplexity and distress, more comfort than any other Bible passage I know. Note first the references to ownership: "My sheep, my voice, I know, me, my hands." Then note the reciprocal relationship of the "owned": "sheep hear, they follow, give unto them eternal life, and they shall never perish." Here we have the great secret of security, both now and in eternity. The Shepherd "owns, calls, gives." The sheep "hear, follow and receive eternal life." And here are the "TWO HANDS": The Jesus hand and the Father hand; the eternal hands of God beneath us to bear us up at all times, and we are safe.

Under the comfort of the above passage many folks, fearing the surgeon's knife, have calmly and trustingly resigned themselves into God's hand and emerged from the operation victorious over disease and doubt. And lo, another miracle had been performed.

REV. F. W. HOFMANN,
York, Pennsylvania.

"Then answered Peter, and said unto Jesus, Lord, it is good for us to be here: if thou wilt, let us make here three tabernacles; one for thee, and one for Moses, and one for Elias."—Matthew 17: 4.

THE Transfiguration of our Lord has a deep significance in its relation to redemption. Peter made the mistake of desiring to spend his life in the joyful light of the mountain-top vision. But our Lord showed him that the vision would mean little or nothing to them and the world unless they should convey it in practical life experience in the valley where sinful, suffering humanity was eagerly awaiting the healing and blessing of the Gospel.

The Church has a mission and a message for the world, and as Christ's messengers, we must perform that mission and deliver that message. There may be a long distance between the mountain-top vision and valley experience, but He commands us to go into all the world and witness for Him.

REV. WILLIAM A. WADE, D.D.,
Baltimore, Maryland.

"Lord, teach us to pray."—Luke 11: 1.

PRAYER is mightier than the sword, slaying the enemies of the soul. Prayer is brighter than the rays of the sun, revealing the hidden depths of the human spirit. Prayer is quicker and stronger than eagles' pinions, bearing us from the atmosphere of earth to the atmosphere of heaven. It is a greater power in the transformation of the world than legislation or force of arms. The center of its power is in the heart which utters it; the radius of its influence is as infinite as the mind of God. It is a snowflake to cool, in a fraction of a second, the fevered brow. It is the lever of Archimedes to move the world.

REV. GEORGE ERNEST MERRIAM, D.D.,
Buffalo, New York.

"Ye have not chosen me, but I have chosen you, and ordained you, that ye should go and bring forth fruit, and that your fruit should remain."—John 15: 16

THE Dean of our Seminary once sent an untried student to the city of New York to be apprenticed to a man of God. Seer and student met in an upper room and in the quiet hour that followed, John 15: 16 became indelibly impressed upon the heart of the student as an all commanding call to service.

Peter and Paul chose fishing and tentmaking respectively as their life work. Christ chose *them* and thereafter fishing and tentmaking became handmaids of Christian service. Peter more than once thought *he* had chosen Christ. The Christ who chooses the lakeside and the rich haul of fishes as a background for a new call to service addressed to Peter chooses your environment as he chooses you.

REV. E. P. PFATTEICHER, D.D., PH.D.,
Philadelphia, Pennsylvania.

"No room for Christ."—Luke 2: 7.

IT IS possible to take a box and fill it with cannon balls so full that you cannot place one more ball. When this has been done you can pour pail after pail of water in, and it will fill up all the vacant space, and not displace a single ball. There was still room for the water.

It is just so with human life. It may be crowded with cares, anxiety, study, work, and the many burdens and responsibilities of life, and yet there should always be room for the inflow of the blessed spirit of Christ. Be sure to give Him first place every day and He will help you in every way. He is not only the great burden bearer but as well the great helper.

REV. D. UPTON BAIR, PH.D.,
Sea Isle City, New Jersey.

"The path of the just is as the shining light, that shineth more and more unto the perfect day."—Proverbs 4: 18.

FIRST comes the hour before the dawn. In nature it is awesome, lonesome, the darkest of the night if we can accept the popular proverb. The hour preceding the awakening of a human soul is likewise dark, lonesome, awesome, filled with struggle and bitter tears.

Next comes the increasing light of dawn. Horizons widen, vision becomes clearer, mists roll away and joy replaces gloom. The widening horizons and increasing light of experience bring a discernment of life's values which always bring forth the same verdict: "Thank God that I chose for Him and the right."

The perfect day! The proof of any process is its finished product. The proof of any life is its close. It is only the godly who can face advancing years with the calm assurance of Robert Browning's words:

"Grow old along with me!
  The best is yet to be,
  The last of life for which the first was made "

REV. JESSE H. BAIRD, D.D.,
Salt Lake City, Utah.

"You have not chosen me, it is I who have chosen you, appointing you to go and bear fruit—fruit that lasts, so that the Father may grant you whatever you ask in my name."—John 15 : 16.   Moffat.

THESE wondrous words spoken by Jesus to His disciples always cause me to rejoice in the glorious privilege of my fellowship in Christ's Church. They bring me high comfort, but they also bring a holy challenge. They take me out into the open fields of my inheritance in Christ, to behold its wide acreages, but they also lead me into the areas of everyday life, and call to honest achievement.

They bring a three-fold message: 1. That Jesus took the initiative, chose me, called me, along with others, to be His. 2. And now, trusting us, He has given us a divine appointment, the fulfillment of which will make us an unfailing source of enrichment to others. 3. And as we fulfill our appointment we open the way for our Heavenly Father to bless the world through us.

REV. E. LE ROY DAKIN, D.D.,
Milwaukee, Wisconsin

"John did no miracle."—John 10: 41.

THE miraculous, romantic and sensational are all about us. Frequently our ideas of greatness are confused with the Wonderful. We wonder, sometimes, how far it is possible to win the Master's approbation without having any power in things miraculous. We live such monotonous and seemingly profitless lives that we do well to remember that Jesus said of John the Baptist that there hath not risen a greater than John the Baptist, yet, "John did no miracle."

It is possible to be true, courageous, self-controlled, sweet, sympathetic, a great soul living a true life, though we do no miracle. Jesus shows here that such lives are frequently used of God to accomplish great results.

Behind men who did great things, are the pious, consecrated mothers who gave themselves in consecration and self-sacrifice—though they did no miracle.

Not brilliancy but faithfulness has the Master's finest approval. "Be thou faithful unto death and I will give thee a crown of life."

REV. EUGENE C. MAKOSKY, D.D.,
Baltimore, Maryland.

"And be not drunk with wine, wherein is excess; but be filled with the Spirit."—Ephesians 5: 18.

TO BE filled with the Spirit is a marvelous provision of divine grace. The fullness of the Spirit is the choicest gift God can give us after we have received Christ, because it is the fullness of God himself who *is* the Spirit.

To be filled with the Spirit is the secret of continual yieldedness to Christ; of a supernatural passion for the unsaved; of a deep love for the Word of God; of a faithful prayer-life; of eager witnessing; of fruitful service and victorious daily living.

But the command of God, that we be filled with the Spirit, is a most sacred obligation as well as a precious privilege. If the will is yielded to obey the command, God surely will fill the believer with Himself.

OLIVER RICHARD HEINZE,
Philadelphia, Pennsylvania.

"And he shall be as the light of the morning, when the sun riseth, even a morning without clouds; as the tender grass springing out of the earth by clear shining after rain."—2 Samuel 23: 4.

LIFE, with all of its experiences of sin, repentance and forgiveness, experiences of failure, struggle and success, of sorrow and joy, despair and glorious victory, has for the man who climbs to the mountain top of spiritual opportunities and blessings, a Christian view of life, a wonderful way of tapering majestically to a glorious and victorious climax.

This is true because the Christian view of life is based upon belief in an infinite God Whose power and love is inexhaustible and Whose effect upon the believer's heart is as "a morning without clouds, when tender grass springeth out of the earth, through clear shining after rain." Especially in these days of bewilderment and distress, men need to obtain the Christian view of life that they may have the heart to keep on climbing toward the summit of the abundant life of glorious victory and eternal triumph.

REV. FLOYD LESLIE BLEWFIELD,
Benton Harbor, Michigan.

"For I determined not to know any thing among you, save Jesus Christ, and him crucified."—1 Corinthians 2:2.

FOR I determined to know nothing among you, save Jesus Christ," and what follows? Here is a coördinate conjunction "And!" And His blameless, beautiful life? And His exalted example? And His ethical teaching? And His sociological program for the human race? No! Not at all! It reads "And Him CRUCIFIED!"

1 Corinthians 1:23 "But we preach Christ CRUCIFIED!"

1 Corinthians 15:3 "For I delivered unto you first of all that which I also received, how that Christ DIED for our sins according to the Scriptures."

The insistent emphasis in the Bible, ever and always, is not upon the birth of Christ, nor upon the life of Christ, but upon the DEATH of Christ; the substitutional, vicarious sacrifice of Christ upon the Cross! "Jesus Christ made peace;" how? "By the blood of His Cross!"

"In the Cross of Christ I glory,
 Towering o'er the wrecks of time;
 All the light of sacred story
 Gathers round Its head sublime!"

REV. W. I. CARROLL, D.D.,
Dallas, Texas.

"As the Father hath loved me, so hath I loved you."
—John 15: 9.

THIS surely is Christ's superlative word concerning His love for His own. The very suggestion fills the soul with the sense of the profoundest depths which cannot be fathomed, with heights that cannot be scaled, with breadths which cannot be encompassed, and of dimensions beyond our knowledge.

"A deep where all our thoughts are drowned."

Two thoughts are immediately suggested; the first, by what He said before; "Therefore doth my Father love Me, because I lay down My life that I may take it again"; and the second, by what He added; "I have kept My Father's commandments, and abide in His Love."

To be worthy of His love we must have His selflessness which suffers to serve, and obey His commandments.

REV. G. CAMPBELL MORGAN, D.D.
Philadelphia, Pennsylvania.

"And for their sakes I sanctify myself, that they also might be sanctified through the truth."—John 17: 19.

HERE the Apostle of love, the spiritual genius of the New Testament breathes into our hearts the spirit of our Blessed Lord.

Would that all Christians realized the need of sanctification as did Christ, the need of sanctification and the need of sanctifying ourselves before we try to sanctify the world.

To make the world good we must be good ourselves. Water does not rise above the level of its own source. Likewise, our influence for good cannot rise above the level of our own Christian living.

This qualification for service can be obtained only in and through Jesus Christ. Our daily contact with Him will consecrate our energies and make us channels of blessing to all about us.

REV. ALFRED J. PENNEY,
Oyster Bay, New York.

"Behold, to obey is better than sacrifice."—1 Samuel 15: 22.

SELF-EXPRESSION is a wonderful thing, but it is not a new invention. Since man staged his first wild and gloating dance of victory before his cave, he has been giving vent to his desire for self-expression. And it helped him to create the tools for his needs.

But he soon learned that individualism had its limits. Power was not forthcoming unless his actions lay along lines that seemed to have been approved without consulting him. Behind everything was a Force which compelled obedience to rules as the price of continued success. Yet obedience irked him, not alone because it was expensive, but chiefly because it put him definitely in second place.

Evasions, magic, cajolery were tried and found wanting. Nothing took the place of obedience. It was this lesson that Samuel taught Saul in the words of our text.

How far has our practical intelligence advanced beyond Saul's?

REV. WALTER C. PUGH, S.T.M.,
Upper Darby, Pennsylvania.

"I counsel thee to buy of me gold tried in the fire, **that** thou mayest be rich."—Revelations 3 : 18.

THIS gold is of the highest possible purity. It contains no alloy, no base metal, or earthly mineral is allowed to lower its divine standard.

To buy it men do not need to sacrifice their honor, or stoop to falsehood and treachery, or betray their manhood. Its possession is not a burden bearing heavily on the soul, like earthly gold, crushing and killing almost every noble and tender feeling of which men and women are capable. It is also a safe investment. Nothing can affect it. Fraud is impossible. Panics though world wide cannot disturb it. Behind it are resources of infinite degree. Buy this gold. It means real wealth. Wealth of character, wealth of splendid manhood, wealth of life crowned with rich and holy service, and as the mines of this gold are inexhaustible, ownership has an assurance that includes worlds unseen and makes possible a life enduring as the ages eternal.

J. WESLEY JOHNSTON, D.D., LITT.D.,
Marion, Massachusetts.

"Enter into thy closet, and when thou hast shut thy door, pray to thy Father which is in secret."—Matthew 6: 6.

IN THE secret place of my heart there is a little door which, if I open and enter, I am in the presence of God. Anywhere, at any time, alone or in the crowded street, in the turning of a thought, I am where God is, rejoicing. When I open the door of prayer, all life has meaning and music; I know without asking; my hunger is fed and my fevered thirst is quenched. The fret and hurry of life are lost in a great quiet; time has melted into eternity. My sorrows flee away like shadows in the dawn, and I see the everlasting hills whence cometh my help. Big things seem small and small things become great; the near is far and the far near. My fellow men are with me in a new intimacy of fellowship, not one forgotten, and those whom I have loved and lost are strangely close and dear when God is near.

REV. JOSEPH FORT NEWTON,
Philadelphia, Pennsylvania.

"Lo, I am with you alway, even unto the end of the world."—Matthew 28:20.

THIS is one of the most precious of the words which fall from the lips of Jesus. It is the assurance of the word of Jesus Himself of His abiding presence in the power and presence of His Spirit. It is a word for believers only. The "alway" or "all of the days," suggests the permanency of His presence all of the days, ranged one after another with all their hours and moments. He enters in and shares with us all the experiences of each day.

We need to make this a fixed maxim, "CHRIST WITH US," so that it shall become a confidence and a conviction upon which time cannot lay its withering hand; no shadow of altered feeling darken it, and no parting hour of last sad farewell, end it. But from eternity to eternity, as yesterday so today, as today so tomorrow, so ever and forever CHRIST WITH US.

REV. LUTHER MOORE BICKNELL,
Goshen, New York.

"In Me ye might have peace."—John 16: 33.

HOW long it took some of us to learn the lesson that there is no peace apart from Christ! We perchance sought it in sinful living only to prove the truth of the Word, "There is no peace saith my God to the wicked." We perhaps endeavored to find it in the paths of worldly pleasure, but had to learn at last in bitter sorrow, "The way of peace have they not known." Or it may be we tried to obtain it by self-righteousness, but found we were only crying "Peace, peace, when there was no peace." At last we came in penitence and faith to Him who by His atoning death "made peace by the blood of His cross," and we learned that "He is our peace" and "being justified by faith we have peace with God." And now as we commit all our affairs to His loving care the "peace of God that passeth all understanding keeps our hearts and minds through Christ Jesus."

REV. H. A. IRONSIDE, LITT. D.,
Chicago, Illinois.

"Thou wilt keep him in perfect peace, whose mind is stayed on thee: because he trusteth in thee."—Isaiah 26: 3.

A RESTLESS world is all about us. I do not refer to the ceaseless urge that gives no rest to solar systems and atoms of the universe. I refer to the busy, craving, straining little mortals that charge the daily life of our western world with anxiety and hurry. They need peace. The message of this verse neutralizes the restlessness and irritation that spoil life for millions. Self-control and serenity are the logical sequences of faith in God. Peace does not come as the result of sheer will power. A thoughtless surrender to fate never produces rest. Men grow hard when subdued into quietude by some cold system of philosophy. It is when faith does its work within that sunlit faces of serene men and women register the reality of that perfect peace to which Isaiah refers.

Rev. William Chalmers Covert, D.D., LL.D.,
Philadelphia, Pennsylvania.

"Verily verily, I say unto you, He that heareth my word, and believeth on him that sent me, hath everlasting life, and shall not come into condemnation; but is passed from death unto life."—John 5 : 24.

DEATH and life are diametrically opposed to each other. The distance between them is immeasurable. By nature we are spiritually dead. No human effort or ingenuity has ever been able to span the distance between death and eternal life. No human power has ever been able to give spiritual life. That which man could not do for himself, God has done for him. God's own Son has provided a divine transition from death to life. The words "is passed" have also been beautifully translated "ferried over." Jesus has ferried us over from the land of death to the land of light and life. This passage across the "Jordan" is a glorious present reality. He has taken us out of the reach of condemnation and ushered us into the place of security. Nothing could be stronger than His own emphatic testimony, "Verily, verily, I say unto you." By His own infinite power and love He has ferried us over the hitherto impassable stream.

REV. ROBERT K. STANSFIELD,
Riverside, New Jersey.

"Save this stranger."—Luke 17: 18.

THE element of surprise in life is one of its best features. It is quite true that it is like a two-edged sword, it cuts both ways. Surprises may shock us as well as assure us.

Jesus could be both shocked and assured. The story of the ten leprous men, only one of whom returned to thank Jesus for healing, reveals this very human trait in His matchless character. Shocked to think that nine of them were so overcome with their own personal gains and interests, yet he was greatly assured to discover that he who returned was an "alien"—a "stranger"—a "Samaritan."

Through each day's experience we will have occasion to be shocked by the ingratitude and coldness of life; but here and there some most unexpected return will buttress our faith in humanity and the finer side of life. There are illimitable possibilities in human nature. Where we least expect it, a "stranger" may remind us that life is worth living.

REV. GEORGE F. FINNIE, D.D.,
Camden, New Jersey.

"I press toward the mark for the prize of the high calling of God in Christ Jesus."—Philippians 3: 14.

ABOVE me and around me lies the unattained.
My spirit longs to walk the beckoning paths.
I fain would run, where now I inch along,
Yet, while I stumble on and drag my feet,
I keep my eyes upon the hill-tops fair,
And take deep breaths of the life-giving air
That comes from those far heights of UN-
    ATTAINED,—
Not what I am but what I will be then
Gives strength, and breathes into my fainting
    soul
The courage that still sends me on, and on,
And steadies me to tread the dusty roads
Which lie between me and the perfect day.

REV. CLARENCE A. VINCENT, D.D.,
Winter Park, Florida.

"See that ye be not troubled."—Matthew 24: 6.

WHAT our Lord really said is made clear in Moffatt's translation: "See, and do not be alarmed." Robert Browning echoes the message in his words: "Trust God; see all, nor be afraid."

Good counsel for anxious times! We need it now, and always.

Some see the disquieting conditions and are alarmed. They lose heart, and give up the fight. Others keep their peace of mind by refusing to face the truth. Jesus calls to the honest, simple, heroic way, of seeing all the facts, and yet keeping a brave heart.

We are living in a disturbed age. Many are fearful and anxious. The Master is calling for many followers who can face the facts without fear, because deep in their hearts is the grace of a living faith, so that they can "see all, and not be afraid."

REV. WILLIAM PIERSON MERRILL, D.D.,
New York City, New York.

"The Lord said . . . I know thee by name. . . . Ther?
is a place by me, and thou shalt stand upon a rock."—
Exodus 33: 17, 21.

MOSES was a very lonely man. He was surrounded by many people yet his life was
solitary and he longed for the assurance that God
cared for him. To this heart-yearning, God gave
the reply of the above Scripture.

Many are asking today, "Does God know ME,
and does He care for ME?" If the answer is
negative, then man may well lose ambition and
hope; but if it is positive, then nothing can daunt
him.

In a universe so large as ours, the Body of man
seems very small indeed and almost insignificant.
but it is man's Soul which justifies God's care.
Because we are made by Him and in His likeness,
we are the objects of His concern.

REV. W. L. ARMSTRONG, D.D.,
Toronto, Ontario, Canada.

"Jesus answered and said unto him, What I do thou knowest not now; but thou shalt know hereafter."—John 13: 7.

SO READS the Authorized Version. The American Revised Version says, "but thou shalt understand hereafter." The English word "know" must do the work of six Greek words and these words have different shades of meaning. The second "know" in John 13: 7 is not the same Greek word as the first "know." The second Greek word means, to come to know, to obtain a knowledge of or insight into. We are in the hands of Fate or Father. These two words have the same letters, excepting that the word Father has two more, but what a difference it makes whether you believe in fate or father. If we are in the hands of our Father, then there is a reason for everything in our lives. Let us patiently wait for what He does. We know not now but we shall come to know hereafter and be satisfied.

REV. HERBERT W. BIEBER, D.D.,
Bala-Cynwyd, Pennsylvania.

"Cast thy bread upon the waters: for thou shalt find it after many days."—Ecclesiastes 11: 1.

IN THE land of Egypt the river Nile overflows its banks in the early summer due to the melting of snow in the highlands of Africa; and as the waters reach the lowlands they flood the level areas far and wide. Whereupon the native farmer scatters seed from a raft which sinks down into the deposit of rich soil from the waters. Then when the waters have passed away, the sunshine quickens the seed into life which is fanned by breezes from the adjoining sea, and the result is the blessing of a rich harvest to be reaped by the sower.

It points us to the waters of life shedding a rich deposit of divine Grace over the areas of our stewardship where sowing the seed of God's love, the rays of the Sun of Righteousness quicken our contributions into new life which is fanned by the Holy Spirit and brings forth much blessing.

REV. P. GEORGE SIEGER, D.D.,
Lancaster, Pennsylvania.

"Is the Spirit of the Lord straitened?"—Micah 2: 7.

THE Holy Spirit desires to *break in* on God's people in gracious reviving power. He would cleanse from all unrighteousness, worldliness, and fleshly energy, perfecting holiness in the fear of God, and bringing into such a oneness with our once crucified, now risen Lord, that He may impart the fullness of His resurrection life and power.

He can then use them in testimony and intercession to *break through* the unbelief, skepticism, and abounding lawlessness; to deliver the prey of the terrible, and the captives of the mighty.

If He thus gains control so that He can work unhindered, He can easily break forth in a great spiritual awakening for our land.

REV. O. R. PALMER,
Philadelphia, Pennsylvania

"As for us, we know the love which God has for us, and we confide in it."—1 John 4: 16. Weymouth.

YOU face the future with hope! Are you confident because your health is good; because you have sufficient financial resources to meet all likely demands; or because you believe that your capabilities will prove as adequate in the future as they have in the past? Each asset is of inestimable value; but about each there is an element of uncertainty. The Christian, while never despising these, has another and underlying ground of confidence, which is the everlasting love of God. Not even upon his love for God does he rely most, for that devotion is not always equally strong. But, come what may, the love of God for him knows no change. On that love he builds his hope and confidence.

"Not what I am, O Lord, but what Thou
　　　art,—
That, that alone can be my soul's true
　　　rest:
Thy love, not mine, bids fear and doubt
　　　depart,
And stills the tempest of my throbbing
　　　breast."

REV. HAROLD W. LANG, M.A., B.D.
Toronto, Ontario. Canada.

"Love Seeketh not its Own."—1 Corinthians 13: 5. Revised Version.

SELFISHNESS seeketh more than its own. It cheats, it robs, it murders, to get what belongs to others. How desolate and desolating is a selfish life. It blights and ruins wherever it rules.

But love, the very essence of God, the expression and manifestation of His being, yields up its own. Christ gives up life itself that a hostile, sinful, selfish world might be saved and filled with bliss. For the joy that was set before Him of bringing many sons to glory He endured the Cross. Love lifts us into fellowship with God. yes, it transforms us into His image and makes us citizens of Heaven.

REV. J. C. KUNZMANN, D.D.,
Seattle, Washington.

"Knock, and it shall be opened unto you."—Luke 11:9.

FAITH is a venture on God that he will do the exact things which he has promised in the Scriptures if you meet his revealed terms. God never gave a single promise to man that is not conditional on the response of the human agent. When he says "Knock, and it shall be opened unto you" he means persistent steadfast knocking until it IS opened. If the door stays fast barred it means that there is something wrong in the knocking. A fireless orthodoxy which rides on an ice-wagon can never save the world. When we meet the terms of prevailing prayer, and the knocking becomes sharp and resonant, Christ's power will move on the midnight sea.

Rev. HENRY McCREA,
Philadelphia, Pennsylvania.

"Love your enemies, bless them that curse you, do good to them that hate you, and pray for them which despitefully use you."—Matthew 5: 44.

THE hardest thing in the world is not to *do* something, but to *be* something. To be something is to live well with others, according to Christ. It is a good thing to live well. It is better to live well with others, but the great achievement comes when one lives well with others, *according to Christ*. This implies love and kindness for foe as well as friend. "For in so doing thou shalt heap coals of fire on his head." This achievement can be reached only by reliance upon Him, of whom Peter said: "Casting all your care upon Him, for He careth for you."

REV. E. ALLEN CHAMBERLIN,
Trenton. New Jersey.

"And when I saw it, I fell upon my face, and I heard a voice of one that spake. And he said unto me, Son of man, stand upon thy feet, and I will speak unto thee."— Ezekiel 1: 28; 2: 1.

STAND upon thy feet!" Surely a strange challenge from the Divine Glory. What should a man do but fall prostrate? Did not the angels veil their faces? What was wrong with Ezekiel?

He was in danger of losing his manhood. An exile, he clung to his fellow-exiles. A believer, his religion was summed up in resignation. His personality was being submerged.

God did not ask Ezekiel to become abject. He was to be responsive, not merely submissive. His individuality was to be God's instrument. Therefore, "Stand upon thy feet."

Each of us must accept responsibility. We must dare as well as endure. God does not save us to diminish personality, but to expand it. There is comfort in His command, "Stand upon thy feet and I will speak unto thee."

REV. R. C. GILLIE, D.C.L., *Bath, England.*

"For ye have not received the spirit of bondage again to fear; but ye have received the Spirit of adoption, whereby we cry, Abba, Father."—Romans 8 : 15.

MUCH of man's religion has been based on fear. The world was peopled with spirits, in earlier times, that have been unfriendly, even hostile. In a more advanced age men have made so many rules and regulations that one cannot move about without infringing these and incurring the penalty of disobedience.

What a different spirit animates those in Christ! Grace supplants law; love banishes fear; the slave is changed into the son. In the hour of Jesus' greatest anguish He could yet look up and cry, "Abba, Father" (Mark 14: 36). And we may be so united with Him, the only Begotten Son, that we may share His spirit of sonship. It will transform life, banish fear, put a new song into our hearts, if at the beginning of each day we but look up and cry, "Abba, Father."

REV. JOHN ABERLY, D.D., *Gettysburg, Pennsylvania.*

"Thy word is a lamp unto my feet."—Psalm 119: 105.

IN EARLY life my Mother gave me a Bible and said, "Son, let this be a lamp unto your feet." It has indeed been a lamp unto my feet. It has been my bread when hungry, my pillow when tired. It has been my inspiration when discouraged, and my joy when sad.

When I think of the testimony of Jesus concerning this Book: its fulfilled Prophecies; the perfect Unity of it, its superiority to any other book, the soundness of its doctrines, the character it produces in those who accept it, as compared with the character of those who reject it. And at last, the testimony of the Soul. I rejoice in the message of God to men. It contains a great height of ideals, a wide range of sympathy, a marvelous reach of aspirations, a fineness of temper and a depth of conviction.

Let it be a lamp unto your feet.

REV. H. FREDERICK JONES,
Baltimore, Maryland.

"He knoweth what is in the darkness."—Daniel 2:22.

READ this chapter of the Book of Daniel and see the dire peril from which the prophet and his companions were delivered by the merciful interposition of God. In his heartfelt thanksgiving Daniel utters the text.

It is a passage fraught with comfort. As we journey along through life how often we are faced with perplexing problems, the solution of which seems impossible. And to us it is impossible. What a comfort then to know that darkness to us means nothing to God and He is our loving Father. His providence is over us. We need but trust in Him and He will see us safely through.

The future, too, is often dark. The more we read the conjectures of men the more confused we become. But the future to God is an open book. He wants us to trust Him. And when we do that we are safe. "I know whom I have believed, and am persuaded that he is able to keep that which I have committed unto him against that day."

REV. ADEN B. MACINTOSH, D.D.,
Lancaster, Pennsylvania.

"For where two or three are gathered together in my name, there am I in the midst of them."—Matthew 18: 20.

THROUGH a crevice in our prison wall we may survey the expanse of heaven; in a moment of time we may enter into and take possession of eternity. And here, in three simple words, we have the unveiled mystery of the Person of Christ. We have the declaration of very Deity, the incommunicable Name, the divine signature, "I AM." We have the omnipresence of the ascended Lord: from generation to generation, in all the centuries, to earth's utmost bound, wherever His people meet to pray, there is He. And to every Christian heart, in each act of devotion, He is the pulse and heart-beat of religious fervor: "Where two or three are gathered together in My Name, there am I in the midst of them."

REV. D. M. M'INTYRE, D.D.,
Glasgow, Scotland.

"And He said unto me, Son of man, can these bones live? . . . And shall put my Spirit in you and ye shall live. . . ."—Ezekiel 37: 3–14.

WHAT a gruesome sight a skeleton is! Yet bones are essential to make a man a man. No hard bones, no fair body.

How attractive is a beautiful body, say, a high school youth flushing with health. What a contrast between such a one and a famine refugee! Yet it takes more than external form and fairness to please God.

A lost child would hardly mistake, for its mother, a model form decked out in the show-window with silk and jewels. It sobs and finds peace and rest only when it lays its head on a heaving bosom underneath which a heart of love beats.

Bones—a body, ah, something lacking yet, 'tis breath. The Breath of God so warm, so loving, so pure, so powerful! I have bones; I may have a fair form, but I absolutely need God's Breath! Oh, how the Christian Church needs the life-giving Holy Spirit of God!

REV. ROY V. DERR,
Woodbury, New Jersey.

"He also that had received two talents came and said,
"Lord, I have gained two other talents beside them."
—Matthew 25:22.

HERE we witness once again that constant
marvel and glory of life, the supreme courage of the average man—the man who refuses
to be upset in character or fidelity to service,
either by the optimism of the five-talented man,
or by the pessimism of the one-talented man. He
invested what he had, he started where he stood.
He was caught between the upper and nether
millstone, but refused to be ground to dust.

Let us thank God for the constructive contribution which the average man makes to the world.
Without him, there could be no armies, industries,
stabilized society, churches and no Kingdom of
God. They present to God and to all true insight of men, the glory of life as they reveal the
supreme dependability and courage of the average man. They not only gain two other talents
also, but better than that, they gain the praise
of the Master Workman Himself.

REV. HARRY CLAYTON ROGERS, D.D.,
Kansas City, Missouri.

"And He said unto them, How is it that ye sought me? wist ye not that I must be about my Father's business?"—Luke 2:49.

JESUS, the Son of God, was always about His Father's business. His Father carried on the greatest international enterprise this world has ever known. This business He has propagated and extended ever since paradise was lost, will not cease until the last soul has been won for heaven.

Jesus was His Father's reliable business-partner. It absorbed His attention from the earliest days of His childhood. It took so firm a grasp on Him that He submitted to ignominious tortures and excruciating pains in body and soul, and finally permitted rude hands of rebellious renegades to rivet Him to the rugged cross. He lived and died in the Father's business, concluding it in this life with those significant words spoken from the cross: "It is finished!"

Have you reported for duty? Have you claimed your share in this great enterprise? Up, and be about the Father's business! It is the Father's business; it is Christ's business; it is your business!

REV. A. M. W. WAHL,
Eau Claire, Wisconsin.

"Be ye therefore perfect."—Matthew 5:48.

A GREEK student, working his way through college, explained: "I make candy. I had a man working for me. He was a bad man. I fired him! A bad man makes bad candy."

A crooked man is crooked in his dealings. And if one is crooked in one field of action, he will be crooked in any other field if an equal opportunity be given to him. Man acts as a unit: if he breaks one law, he becomes guilty of the whole law. My religion is shown by my life. Morality is bound to religion: in both, it is the whole man that functions.

"Be ye therefore perfect."

Ross Miller, Ph.D.,
Springfield, Ohio.

"My word . . . shall not return unto me void, but it
shall accomplish that which I please, and it shall prosper
in the thing whereunto I send it."—Isaiah 55: 11.

SHARPER than any two-edged sword, a dis-
cerner of the thoughts and intents of the
heart," inspired by God, sent forth by God, His
Word can be depended upon from Genesis to Revelation. And if you will use it in dependence
upon the Holy Spirit, that Word will work miracles in human lives; for it is the instrument used
of God in the regeneration and purification of the
soul.

"Of making many books there is no end," but
the philosophies and theories of men, like themselves, are of short duration. The Apostle tells
us (1 Peter 1: 22–25) that the Word of God, like
Himself, is incorruptible, alive, life-begetting and
imperishable. "The Word of the Lord endureth
forever. And this is the Word which by the
Gospel is preached unto you."

REV. MERRIL THOMAS MACPHERSON,
Philadelphia, Pennsylvania.

"But godliness with contentment is great gain."—1 Timothy 6: 6.

A PERSON who believes in Christ and lives his faith has no wants. He seeks no occasion to exploit his fellowmen. Neither is he exposed to the temptations and snares into which wealth often lures its owners. His daily supplies are drawn from God's bountiful stores. He is content with adequate food, clothing and shelter, for he knows that the excesses of the rich only bring misery upon them. Besides, he is free from the cares and anxieties that continually harass the ungodly. Therefore, the Christian is more at ease with what God allows him, than the covetous can ever hope to be with all their ill-gotten gain. Godliness and contentment bring peace and happiness to the soul. What more can one want?

REV. CHARLES E. KISTLER, D.D.,
Reading, Pennsylvania.

"Turn you to the strong hold, ye prisoners of hope."— Zechariah 9 : 12.

WHAT is the basis of the experience of good men and women of the Christian ages, regardless of what official creed they have held? Has it been the conviction that they were orphans, alone, deserted, in an insensate universe? No! It has been the conviction that our puny efforts to bring in the reign of justice and peace are sustained by something in the structure of the universe itself; that truth and right have the universe on their side. It is a heroic faith which holds that humanity must fight its battles alone, but it is no more heroic than the faith, based on Christian experience, that the stars in their courses fight against wrong. Such faith leaves us no longer prisoners except in the sense that we are spell-bound by the possibilities, yet unrealized, of our partnership with the Eternal. We are prisoners of hope."

REV. OSCAR EDWARD MAURER, D.D.,
New Haven, Connecticut.

"For I do always those things that please him."—John 8:29.

IN THIS verse of Scripture we find the motive by which Jesus ruled His life. And since He spoke them Himself, we have the best warrant for believing He ruled His life by that motive: *to please God.* If what He did and the way He did it was intended to give His Heavenly Father pleasure, then it becomes increasingly clear that the Christian can do no less than govern his life by this principle that gives peace and poise to the development of the inner life and to its outward expression. A service rendered to the most unworthy, "for God's sake," can be performed with pleasure. A sacrifice made for those least appreciative, can be made with joy. "Inasmuch as ye have done it unto the least, ye have done it unto me." What an inspiration to all of God's people, if we tried daily to please our Heavenly Father.

REV. AUGUST POHLMAN, D.D., M.D.,
Philadelphia. Pennsylvania.

"In all thy ways acknowledge Him, and He shall direct thy paths."—Proverbs 3:6.

THE offer of Divine guidance appeals to the deepest cravings of the human soul. It is conditional; we must "acknowledge Him in all our ways." That is, acknowledge His *right* to direct us: this implies absolute surrender of ourselves to God for His purposes; acknowledge His *ability* to direct us: this implies the possibility for us of noble aspirations, wise judgments, and right decisions; acknowledge God's infinite *willingness* to direct us: this implies our loving trust and eager seeking.

Such is the attitude of those who "walk with God"; who, "beholding His glory are changed into His image" and become "lights in the world; who set up right standards of truth and justice; and bring in the reign of peace and goodwill among men."

REV. GEORGE WELLS ELY,
New Rochelle, New York.

"Follow thou me."—John 21: 22.

THIS is the word of our Lord repeated, on the eve of His departure from the sight and touch of His disciples. It was apparently His common word to people, to the young ruler, to the man who wanted to go and say farewell to his friends —and to many others—equivalent to His other great words, "Believe on me."

You can pray to Him to be made aware of His presence. You can touch Him in life's thorny places. You can receive of His fullness in the common work of today. The whole scenery in living is compressed into these two words. They are vital and comprehensive. First and last, in the morning and evening of life, after failure and shameful sin, Jesus says to you, "Follow thou me." What will be your response today? "Lord, I will follow Thee."

REV. CHARLES BROWN, D.D.,
Herts, England.

"Lo, I am with you alway, even unto the end of the world."—Matthew 28: 20.

WHAT a comforting promise! Jesus is going away from his disciples, yet, they are not to be lost sight of; leaving them, He will be with them as much as He was with Peter on the water or with the friends at Bethany. Alone: never.

A most wonderful promise! Too great for these disciples to comprehend, yet their experience, as all other religious experiences, leads to the confession, "Thou are with me."

A child about to undergo an operation is mysteriously comforted with the assurance that his father will stand by him, so the Lord cheers with the promise of His personal presence in all the vicissitudes of life. The Hebrew children in the fiery furnace had One like the Son of man with them.

An orphan, facing temptation, conscious of God's presence, in the language of another, "How can I do this thing and sin against God," conquered. In the hour of loneliness, when none seemed to care, the assurance of His fellowship cheered; He encouraged and sent on to labor rejoicing; when life's pilgrimage is ended, one shall lie down in peace because "Thou art with me." This is the promise which makes life victorious.

REV. ULYSSES E. APPLE, D. D.,
Annville, Pennsylvania.

"We know that all things work together for good to them that love God."—Romans 8:28.

THINGS seen separately may not always appear to be working for our good. It is much as when we observe the items of litter that always accompany building. Viewed apart, the box for mixing mortar, and the yard for the broken chips of stone, do not appear kindly. Yet they do at last "work together" in the building of grace and comfort. Too often we see life in its fragments, as we look forward; but when we look backward it is surprising to note how things, apparently hostile, have been parts of a kindly and providential program.

The condition is located in ourselves. We would expect the wording: "To them that God loves." Instead of this, our love toward God is the condition, as His love toward us is surely fixed and unfailing.

Try the promise, under the light of these two suggestions; and then judge whether its deep and inner meaning has been met in your lives.

RT. REV. EDWIN H. HUGHES,
Chicago, Illinois.

"My God, my God, why hast Thou forsaken Me?"—Mark 15:34.

WHERE WAS GOD WHEN HIS SON WAS DYING? HAD HE FORSAKEN HIM? Was he dwelling in some shining city beyond the stars? No, not that! He had come so close that never more need He be sought. Where was God? Why God was the Vision for which Jesus was dying. God was the Light which led Him into the Lonely Land and which He would not desert though Heaven forsook Him. God was the Love for which He climbed to the Cross. God was the Prayer "Father forgive them." Jesus was not forgotten. He was dwelling in the inmost secret of the Father's Soul.

And we are not forsaken when we climb great gray hills of grief. God is the Patience distilled from pain; God is the Sympathy born of Sorrow; God is the Faithfulness learned in unromantic toil and task. God is the Holy Impatience which, beholding triumphant Evil, cries, "My God— why?" God is the Star which shines through rifted storm clouds of Death.

Often when we feel most forsaken, we are nearest God.

REV. WILLIAM HENRY BODDY,
Chicago, Illinois.

"His head and his hairs were white like wool, as white as snow; and his eyes were as a flame of fire."—Revelation 1: 14.

W E MUST learn to face our problems, not only on the levels of life, but in the light that streams from the Eternal.

The image in which the vision is clothed tells us of the Sovereign Majestic Christ. We see Jesus, the Eternal High Priest, Whose unceasing intercession for men proclaims to us that our needs and our aspirations are known to God.

He is ever young with the youth of love, sympathy and purpose, to help us meet the needs of the new day. He gives us the authoritative word about life. As well attempt to silence the waves or the waterfall, as to gainsay the appeal of Jesus Christ to faith and to conscience.

Those faithful to Him, He keeps. He holds the stars. The Church is safe in His Hands. I am safe in His Hands.

God reigneth, be the earth never so unquiet.

To serve the Sovereign Christ is the way of victory and peace.

VERY REV. L. W. B. BROUGHALL, D.D.,
Hamilton, Ontario, Canada.

"Stand still, and see the salvation of the Lord."—Exodus 14:13.

THESE words are from Moses, God's chosen leader, who was to deliver His people from their Egyptian bondage. What a predicament they were in at this time. There stood the hosts of Israel, before them the mighty waters of the Red Sea, behind them the pursuing hordes of the Egyptian army. They were caught—helpless! For them the dark clouds of terror were gathering. In this hour of their distress Moses cried unto them, "Fear not, stand still and see the salvation of the Lord." That night God took the east wind, and lifted up the waters of the Red Sea, making a passage of escape, and His people crossed in safety, delivered from their enemies!

Is your heart burdened down with sorrow? Does everything seem to be going against you? Do you feel yourself hopelessly defeated? Is there nothing but ruin and disaster ahead? "Stand still, and see the salvation of the Lord." Be calm, quiet. Trust the Lord, and watch Him deliver you, in a marvelous way. "He will not fail thee nor forsake thee."

REV. RALPH E. WALLIS,
Philadelphia, Pennsylvania.

"Commit thy way unto the Lord; trust also in him; and he shall bring it to pass."—Psalms 37: 5.

DISHEARTENED over the seeming impossibilities of establishing a church in the town where I had labored for months, I was seated in a train speeding eastward over the Colorado plains to a town where I hoped to locate in a more promising field.

A man passed through the coach and handed a piece of literature to each passenger. The card he gave me bore the following lines:

"Make a little fence of trust around today,
  Fill the space with loving works and
      therein stay;
  Look not through the sheltering bars
      upon tomorrow,
  God will help thee bear what comes, if
      joy or sorrow."

This message made me see God's love and care more clearly; and I returned next day, and success came out of seeming failure. The name of the messenger was never known to me.

REV. P. E. BIERBAUER,
Philadelphia, Pennsylvania.

"Be thou my strong habitation, whereunto I may continually resort: thou hast given commandment to save me; for thou art my rock and my fortress."—Psalms 71:3.

HERE is voiced the deep cry of the soul. For there come times to every one when the soul needs a refuge. Self-help fails; human and worldly help are insufficient. God is the only hope and help. In almost despair and yet in trust the soul throws itself on God, crying, "Be thou my strong habitation—my Rock of habitation—my fortress and dwelling-place,—to which I may continually resort," and hide myself in Thy Divine security.

When doubts and temptations torment the soul; when cares and anxiety consume the mind; when sickness and losses depress the spirit; when enemies annoy; when old age with its infirmities steals upon us; when proverty threatens; what comfort and strength to know that there is a Strong Habitation; that God has given commandment to save us; that He is our Refuge and Strength.

REV. CHARLES STORK JONES, M.A.,
Dorby, Pennsylvania.

"But when he saw the multitudes, he was moved with compassion on them, because they fainted, and were scattered abroad, as sheep having no shepherd. Then saith he unto his disciples, The harvest truly is plenteous, but the labourers are few."—Matthew 9: 36, 37.

THE Bible abounds in passages that are precious because of the comfort they bring and the service they inspire. But as I advance in age and experience, I find myself, with an aching, breaking heart, repeating within the depths of my own spiritual being, the above passage perhaps more than any other. As I contact the world, in all its complicated relationships, I am increasingly impressed that multitudes of them are "Like sheep having no shepherd." They have lost the way, and unless we have compassion on them, they will never find the way home; the way of truth and beauty; of peace and joy; the Father's way as revealed in our Lord and Master. It is compassion, not criticism, that is going to transform the world. No matter how few we can help, we must want to help all, with a great yearning desire that amounts to compassion, or the task will never be accomplished. "He was moved with compassion on them, as sheep having no shepherd."

REV. FRANK G. SMITH,
Omaha, Nebraska.

"And because ye are sons, God sent forth the Spirit
of his Son into your hearts, crying, Abba, Father."—
Galatians 4: 6.

THE Scriptures tell us *who we are*. *We are children of God*. By all the mystery of our
coming into the world, we are children. We came
from God. He sent us. He claims us. He owns
us. But this sonship has become sadly dwarfed.
Yet, however ruined a man's life may be, he was
still sent by God. God gave him his being.

Our sonship which has fallen so far short of
what sonship ought to be is given back to us.
Christ does that for us in his *redeeming* work.
Christ Jesus the Son, who took upon himself our
nature and become man, came to restore us to a
new and complete sonship. That is the burden
of the New Testament.

How should a child of God live? What should
he be like? A good child of God should have
love, joy, peace, long suffering, kindness, goodness, faithfulness, meekness, self-control. The
Spirit of his Son in our hearts gives us that true
kind of sonship.

REV. L. H. LARIMER, D.D., LL.D.,
Springfield, Ohio.

"Unto the upright there ariseth light in the darkness."
—Psalms 112 : 4.

THIS is a sure word of prophecy and of such measure of comfort as to cover the petty uncertainties of the daily round and the graver experiences of bewilderment that are sure to befall us. The ring of confidence in the words suggests that the message is born of experience and observation.

The promise, however, is to the upright, and not those who merely conform to acknowledged standards of rectitude. They are the upright in heart, selfless in purpose and pure, with singleness of aim. These are in the most favorable condition for divine illumination. Did not the Master say, "Blessed are the pure in heart, for they shall see God"? Without the distraction of self-seeking or self-vindication we are best prepared to discover the gleam and as in life we go step by step we must not look for light before the time but in confidence possess our souls and press on.

REV. W. M. ROCHESTER, D.D.,
Toronto, Ontario, Canada.

"Blessed are they that have not seen, and yet have believed."—John 20: 29.

LIFE'S heaviest loss is a believing heart. In this Beatitude of the Believers the Master declares the happiness of trustful disciples. Thomas was the Knight-Errant of Doubting Castle. He was a reluctant skeptic. His doubt and its cure have healed many a troubled spirit. For the sake of Christian Evidences we rejoice in this cypress-tree rationalist.

"Doubt is a reasonable pause before the unknown." It may be honest. The sincere man cries: "Lord, I believe; help Thou mine unbelief." The Master dealt tenderly with honest doubters. Not so with Pharisees!

What, then, shall we do with doubt? With open mind and prayerful spirit, in secret sanctuary, study the Words of Jesus. Thus many a baffled spirit has come to soul rest and quenched his thirst after the Eternal. A major need of our time is mental rest—soul healing.

REV. G. BICKLEY BURNS, D.D.,
Philadelphia, Pennsylvania.

"Lord, what wilt thou have me to do?"—Acts 9: 6.

THIS should be the key-note to the Christian's life-service. When love comes into the heart it spontaneously expresses itself in service. Saved by faith—faith begets love and love quickens an urge to service. This is a natural sequence, an inevitable process. Sin, salvation, service, the triad of Christian experience.

A tree bears fruit from the fullness of a normal life, it cannot do otherwise; so the Christian bears the fruit of a consecrated life—a life full of love—he just cannot do otherwise. That fruit is service.

There is a greater need than ever for Christian service and the opportunities are on every hand; daily they are evident; we need but look about us; they are with us—at our very door.

REV. SYDNEY E. BATEMAN, M.D., Sc.D.
Margate City, New Jersey.

"What shall I render unto the Lord for all his benefits toward me?"—Psalms 116: 12.

GOD LOVED me. He gave his all for me, His only begotten Son, that I might be saved.

Jesus suffered, bled and died upon the cross for me. He conquered sin, death and the devil, in order that I might have life and have it more abundantly. The Holy Spirit calls me through Christ's gospel and keeps me in this blessed faith. Loved, redeemed, sanctified by God. Not only that, but this wonderful God daily supplies all my needs.

How then do I treat Him? I may treat Him like a beggar, into whose tin cup I cast a pittance. Like employer to employee. Discharge him, if I have no need for Him. Like a Partner! I would not think of appropriating that, which rightly belongs to my partner. Without God, My Partner, I can do nothing. I will give Him my heart, my time, my means, my life, my all.

REV. OSCAR J. WARNATH,
Philadelphia, Pennsylvania.

"And the Lord said unto David my father, Whereas it was in thine heart to build an house unto my name, thou didst well that it was in thine heart."—1 Kings 8: 18.

I BELIEVE the road to Heaven is paved with good intentions. I believe that the Eternal City will be inhabited by people who, during their earthly career, had high Christian ideals and noble Christlike aims. Such aspirations are essentials to progress and achievement.

But, suppose the goal is never reached, the intention never fulfilled. Has the mental activity been in vain—a total loss? The Lord answers our question by the words, "Thou didst well that it was in thine heart." He appreciates our high ambitions and rejoices in our good desires even though they are not fulfilled.

Think also of the indirect practical value of a high ambition. He who would build a chapel can realize his aims, but he who planned the Cathedral of Cologne, the building of which required six centuries, would not see his dream come true.

REV. A. H. KLEFFMAN,
Wilmington, Delaware.

"Remember Jesus Christ."—2 Timothy 2:8. American Version.

THIS is Paul's farewell to Timothy. Instead of a "forget-me-not" he sends the lovelier bloom of self-forgetful faith, the very flower of Pauline thought: "remember-Jesus-Christ." Such a blossom, from Paul's hand, has a rare delicacy not cultivated in the garden of Jesus' physical fellowship, but grown rather in the actinic spiritual radiance of the "Sun of Righteousness."

To remember is to recall one already known. Paul and Timothy were sure they knew Jesus, though never having seen Him in the flesh. If we dwell as consciously as they in the fellowship of Christ's spirit, we too will breathe forth the fragrance of such a flower.

This verse whispers searchingly: "You know Christ. Remember Him in your thought. You love Christ. Remember Him winsomely to His friends. You trust Christ. Remember Him daily in your living will, persuaded 'that He is able to guard that which you have committed unto Him against that day.'"

REV. WILLIAM HORATIO PHELPS, D.D.,
Des Moines, Iowa.

"He knoweth the way that I take: when he hath tried me, I shall come forth as gold."—Job 23: 10.

THERE is truth in the statement that history and civilization are the composite of the individual. Certainly the history of the race repeats itself in the experience of most of us. This philosophy of trouble bearing which has come down to us from the ancient is a wonderful source of comfort for us as individuals. Every life has its course in which strain and stress is mingled, sometimes apparently meaninglessly. Trials of one kind or another come to every human being. No human way has ever been devised to avoid them. How strengthening then to be able to say "He knoweth!" The inspired book is replete with promises that our trials will never be more than we can bear. "He knoweth!" It would be well for us to learn the patience of confidence in Him, to practice the stimulating belief that trials will end and ending will be found to have contributed richly to the character.

REV. VICTOR ALEXANDER RULE, D.D.,
Phœnix, Arizona.

"In nothing be anxious; but in every thing by prayer and supplication with thanksgiving let your requests be made known unto God. And the peace of God, which passeth all understanding, shall guard your hearts and your thoughts in Christ Jesus."—Philippians 4: 6, 7. Revised Edition.

THE child is careless. The man is careful. The saint is carefree. Such peace is beyond the reaches of reason. Peace is pardon. Peace is the friendship of God. Peace is the gentleness of love, breathing good will. Peace is the calm of a trusting child of God in the storms and griefs of life. Peace is the quiet assurance of the Christian pilgrim journeying by whatever road to the city of God. Peace is tranquillity in the valley of the shadow of death. Peace is the greeting of Jesus at the gates of pearl. Peace is the Rest that remaineth for the people of God.

REV. GEORGE N. LUCCOCK, D.D.,
Wooster, Ohio.

"I am come that they might have life, and that they might have it more abundantly."—John 10: 10.

ABOVE everything else man has wanted full-ness of life. He has sought this goal in many ways. Socrates sought it through wisdom. Michael-Angelo through art; and Nero through his beastly debaucheries. Today we seek it through pleasure, or profit, or power.

Christ has the answer. Christ was interested in man's physical life and healed the sick and cleansed the leper. He was interested in man's mental life and confounded the wise men of His day with His own wisdom. He was interested in man's social life and shared in it. But above all He was interested in enriching man's soul. By bringing to man's soul His own spirit, Christ has brought abundance into the lives of all those Who receive Him.

REV. CLIFFORD E. BARBOUR, PH.D.,
Knoxville, Tennessee.

"Jesus said unto him, Thou shalt love the Lord thy God with all thy heart, and with all thy soul, and with all thy mind. This is the first and great commandment. And the second is like unto it, Thou shalt love thy neighbor as thyself."—Matthew 22: 37–39.

PERPLEXED, but serious-minded persons, seeking to learn the secret of right living, turn to the words of Jesus for instruction. Some real disappointment is suffered when they fail to find an elaborate set of rules for living. He who rightly discerns the Mind of the Master rejoices when he appreciates to the full the meaning of these wonderful words. Jesus Christ does not burden us with elaborate rules of conduct but He has given us a Principle of Living. This is the Principle of Love which He directs us to apply to two objectives: first, to the Lord our God, and so become spiritualized; secondly, to our fellow men, and so become socialized. The first is demonstrated in the second; the second is never possible unless the first is realized.

REV. ROBERT FORTENBAUGH, PH.D.,
Gettysburg, Pennsylvania.

"And will be a Father unto you, and ye shall be my sons and daughters, saith the Lord Almighty."—2 Corinthians 6: 18.

ON THIS promise those who have given themselves to godliness and committed their affairs to divine guidance may face life's conditions, temptations and duties knowing that God will give to them what children have a right to expect from an ideal Father.

They may expect in days of need from the Heavenly Father parental guardianship by way of provision, "But my God shall supply all your *need* according to his riches in glory by Christ Jesus." And by way of protection, "For the eyes of the Lord run to and fro throughout the whole earth to show himself *strong* in the behalf of them whose heart is perfect toward him."

They may expect in days of sorrow parental comfort, "As one whom his mother comforteth, so will I comfort you."

In these days when the heart craves enjoyment they may expect parental entertainment, "In thy presence is fullness of joy and at thy right hand pleasures forevermore."

With such assurances the changes in circumstances may be faced knowing that the Heavenly Father careth for His own.

REV. CHARLES M. BOSWELL, D.D.,
Philadelphia, Pennsylvania.

"As thy days, so shall thy strength be."—Deuteronomy
33 : 25.

HERE is a word from God with promise and
power. It comes with meaning, new every
morning, to all believers—to the youth with les-
sons or labors before him; to the aged, lingering
in leisure; to the sick in home or hospital as well
as the physically fit, with burdens heavy to bear;
to the poor with meager supply and the rich in
their abundance. All may claim the promise and
receive its power.

All conditions are included. "As thy days"—
whatever the prospects or problems; serious questions to be decided, ominous messages to be received, monotonous work or weary waiting, sickness or sorrow, depressing defeat or exultant victory. In every experience, no exceptions, God
has promised strength according to the need.
Paul knew its meaning when he said, "I can do
all things through Christ who strengtheneth me."

REV. ELBERT HEFNER, D.D.,
Fort Smith, Arkansas.

"In all their affliction, he was afflicted, and the angel of his presence saved them: in his love and in his pity he redeemed them."—Isaiah 63 : 9.

NOTHING is harder to bear than to be misunderstood. It is hard enough to be misunderstood by our friends. And there is no time when we are in more danger of misunderstanding the best of all friends than when our eyes are filled with tears of sorrow. This was the mood of the two disciples on their way to Emmaus, when their Lord came to them and showed them that He was never nearer to them, or doing so much for them, as when they thought He had failed them.

The mystery of pain and suffering has always been hard to understand. Even our Savior, when bearing our sins and sorrows when the Father's face was turned away, cried out "My God, my God, why?" Nor can the "thorn in the flesh" always be removed, even in answer to prayer. But He knows how much we can bear, and says, "My grace is sufficient for you."

REV. W. D. STRANGEWAY,
Watervliet, New York.

"Philip saith unto him, Lord, show us the Father, and it sufficeth us."—John 14: 8.

THE deepest need of the human heart is to find God, the Father. In numerous ways the world over, man is asking Philip's question, "Show us the Father." God knew of that longing, and took the most effective way of satisfying it. He sent His son Jesus Christ into the world to reveal Him to men, and show the world that He is and what He does.

Jesus fed the hungry, He relieved suffering, He visited homes where death had broken family circles, and He shared the sorrows of the bereaved ones. His marvelous life is beautifully epitomized by the sacred writer, "He went about doing good."

Thus we see in Jesus that God our Father is interested in all the details of our daily lives. We may tell Him everything, we may trust Him everywhere. He is our Father and He will not disappoint us.

REV. GEORGE M. BELL,
Johnson City, New York.

"In your patience ye shall win your souls."—Luke 21: 19. Revised Version.

THE tendency with most of us is to get all out of patience with God and to feel that He needs us in the running of the world. But it is the part of those who really believe God rules to look out upon our confused life with calm eyes. Human nature is often stubborn. The road to ideals is longer than we think. It takes time to bring worthy things to pass. It takes God time to do things. He's been working on us, human, through generations and centuries, yet see what we are. He'll need longer still to bring us to what He'd have us to be. Who are we, then, that we should be in a hurry? We are to be patient with ourselves. To hold on is to win.

REV. GEORGE W. C. HILL,
New Britian, Connecticut.

"Let this mind be in you, which was also in Christ Jesus."—Philippians 2: 5.

CHRISTIAN humility and meekness always go with a full conception of the majesty and purpose of the Christian life.

His true conception of His mission to save and serve, His poise, patience, self composure, and sympathy, is an illumination and helpful to all. Perfectly conscious of the fullness of the Godhead dwelling in Him, He might, humanly speaking, have been tempted to display it in answer to the frequent challenges of Satan, "If Thou be the Son of God." However our Lord's mind was of different temper. The words of St. Paul's show "Who being in the form of God thought it not a thing to be grasped after to be equal with God, but made Himself of no reputation, and took upon himself the form of a servant and was obedient even unto the death on the Cross." This mind should and can be in us The Inspiration of His example and the power of His Spirit alone can accomplish this for those who sincerely desire to be like Him. Let us not only adore Him but grow unto his likeness!

REV. GEORGE A. GREISS, D.D.,
Allentown, Pennsylvania.

"Thou wilt keep him in perfect peace, whose mind (thought, imagination, heart) is stayed on thee."—Isaiah 26: 3.

A HUMAN life, in its natural course, must face ever-changing problems, and often they are or seem baffling. Must one, then, yield to doubts and fears? Or, may his life be free from anxiety (Mark 7: 34). May one's life move on with persistent steadfastness (1 Corinthians 15: 58) yet with peace like a river (Isaiah 66: 12)—a river whose surface is ruffled by boisterous winds but whose whole volume moves quietly, calmly, but ever onward toward its ocean home?

By grace such a peace may be his whose mind is stayed on God, our Father in Heaven Who loves as only a heavenly Father can love.

REV. FRANK P. MANHART, D.D., LL.D.,
Selinsgrove, Pennsylvania.

"Worthy is the Lamb."—Revelation 5 : 12.

THE Lamb that was slain." Heaven does not erase those wounds so reminiscent of the dark night of His agony. Even when I reach the land of endless day, I shall be perpetually reminded that I owe all to Him who died for me on Calvary.

The highest place that heaven affords, is His by sovereign right. The head that once was crowned with thorns is crowned with glory now. How it cheers me amid the tempests and trials of life to know that all power is His—to succor and sustain.

"The Lamb shall overcome them." It is the assurance that the final rout of all my foes is certain. One glad day I shall stand secure in the frowning triumph of the Lord of Glory. He Who is in me is greater than all who can be against me. "Verily, the Lamb is all the glory in Immanuel's Land!"

REV. W. M. ROBERTSON,
Vancouver, British Columbia, Canada.

"The Lord is my shepherd . . . and I will dwell in the house of the Lord for ever."—Psalm 23: 1–6.

THIS psalm answers three real and present fears of man—the fears of poverty, loneliness and evil. Because men fear poverty, they are tempted to worry, to lie, to steal, and commit great crimes in order to escape it. "I shall not want" is the Lord's answer and the Christians' faith.

Because men fear loneliness, they are tempted to promote questionable companionships, lower their standards, surrender their convictions and follow the crowd. "Thou art with me," assures a soul-satisfying companionship.

Because men fear evil, they are tempted to worship the god of things as they are, to stoop to the cowardice of side-stepping in the face of clear duty, and to play safe when confronted by moral decisions. "I will fear no evil, thou art with me," is the soul's tonic. The place of safety is where God is.

These are practical tests of faith in the Lord our Shepherd.

REV. FREDERICK W. MEYER,
Camden, New Jersey.

"Wherefore take unto you the whole armor of God, that ye may be able to withstand in the evil day, and, having done all, to stand."—Ephesians 6: 13.

HAVING done right and also done wrong, your wrongdoing so far exceeding your rightdoing that life seems wrecked; whatever the failure, stand. The easier way would be to run from the consequences. That way is cowardly.

God describes Himself as Shield and Buckler. The Armour of God is God himself, for God is armour incarnate. People incarnate a portion only. Some one piece, some another.

It may be said with assurance that no one has lived among people without making friends. Some of your friends incarnate God's armour. One strong to speak a true word, another strong in faith, another to do the right thing. Clothe yourself with them, and hold the good ground left to you. You will regain more ground as you stand.

REV. GEORGE McNEELY, D.D.,
Newark, New Jersey.

"For he shall give his angels charge over thee, to keep thee in all thy ways."—Psalms 91: 11.

THE Christian religion is positive as to spiritual realities. From Genesis to Revelation, "angels" and other spirits, good and evil, are seen to cross the human path and, as with magic touch, help shape the course of history. Eliminate spirits and the spiritual from the Bible and there remains but an empty shell.

Do we in the darkness confidently sing?
> "Through the long night-watches
>   May Thine angels spread,
>   Their white wings above me,
>   Watching round my bed."

May we pray daily in the Vesper petition:

"Let Thy holy angel have charge concerning us, that the wicked one have no power over us."

Above all, may we take seriously God's promise:

"The angel of the Lord encampeth round about them that fear Him and delivereth them."

REV. J. WLLIAM McCAULEY,
Baltimore, Maryland.

"Beloved, now are we the sons of God, and it doth not yet appear what we shall be: but we know that, when he shall appear, we shall be like him; for we shall see him as he is."—I John 3 : 2.

NO MATTER how dark the day; no matter how troubled we are; how many times we have failed; no matter how futile and useless life seems to us; our salvation is in the great truth that God has revealed to us in Jesus Christ, that we are indeed sons of God, not in our past, not in time to come, but even now, in our weakness and failure. We cannot see how it is to be, yet we know that we shall be like the perfect Son of Man. Nothing can separate us from the love of God and nothing can deprive us of our ultimate end. We are sons of the Highest Power and Strength, we are God's own children, and our progress is sure if we can only remember who and what we are. As we keep this in mind, we shall cease to fear and we shall know that there is but one reality. That reality is Life. There is but one life. That life is continuous and continuously good. It comes from God, the giver of all good gifts. God is our Father. It doth not yet appear what we shall be, but we know that we shall be like Him.

REV. RANDOLPH RAY, D.D.,
New York City, New York.

"There is therefore now no condemnation to them which are in Christ Jesus."—Romans 8: 1.

TO ANY sincere Christians who, at any particular time, may not be just sure of their standing before God, these words of St. Paul carry an assuring message. We never need doubt the certainty of our salvation. But how may I know, at any time, that my salvation is sure? By this: "If we confess our sins, he is faithful and righteous to forgive our sins, etc." Now if, as opportunity is afforded, I confess my sins and ask for forgiveness, and believe Christ's promise, and at all times my attitude of mind and heart toward God is one of confession and desire for forgiveness, by Christ's own promise I have forgiveness. Therefore I am always free from condemnation of sin. I am living under justification, not because I deserve it, but because God for Jesus Christ's sake freely grants it unto me.

Rev. David S. Hafer,
Phillipsburg, New Jersey.

"Thou wilt keep him in perfect peace, whose mind is stayed on thee: because he trusteth in thee."—Isaiah 26: 3.

CHRIST assumed the divine obligation of this verse when He said: "My peace I give unto you. Let not your heart be troubled, neither let it be fearful." The chief obstacle to peace is sin. Hence we pray: "O Lamb of God, Who takest away the sins of the world, grant us Thy peace." The daily disturbers of our peace are the anxieties that crowd upon our imaginative minds. Trust in God is the antidote. Christ's keeping our minds in peace depends upon our staying our minds on Him in trust. The secret of serenity is the habit of relying upon Jesus; always in little matters, that we may be prepared for great necessities. The peace will be perfect in proportion as our trust is absolute.

RT. REV. LEWIS W. BURTON, D.D., *Lexington, Kentucky.*

"In my Father's house are many rooms."——John 14: 2.
Goodspeed's Version.

IT IS a comfort to think of our dear ones who
have passed on, as being merely in another
room of the Father's house, with only a curtain
between us.

This curtain was drawn aside on the Mount of
Transfiguration when the Christ stepped through
the door and talked with Moses and Elijah, dis-
cussing the problem of death with radiant faces.

The curtain fell back: the disciples lived once
more in this prosaic world: they never forgot
the vision.

What they saw for a moment gives us faith to
believe that no time or space can separate us
from those we love, when all are one in Christ,
"of whom the whole family in heaven and earth
is named."

REV. GEORGE E. TALMAGE,
Oyster Bay, New York.

"My help cometh from the Lord, which made heaven and earth."—Psalm 121: 2.

I HAD just turned into my twentieth year. Hundreds of miles from home, I was a stranger in a strange city. I had taken a good position in a clothing store and started in to make my way in the world. I was stricken with typhoid fever and taken to a hospital where I lay for nine weeks.

One Sabbath afternoon, discouraged beyond discription, I lay homesick and ready to give up the fight, as the Doctors had held out little hope. A young man approached my bed and spoke. He opened his Bible and read to me from various Scriptures. At last he turned to the 121st Psalm and read it. It struck home to my heart in all its graciousness, hope revived. That night the Doctor noted a change. My conversion took place quietly, the way opened to the ministry. The Scripture has always been precious to me. It will be to you.

REV. DAVID T. ROBERTSON, D.D.,
Marshfield, Oregon.

"A word fitly spoken is like apples of gold in pictures of silver."—Proverbs 25: 11.

IN A church in Philadelphia, a boy of four-teen rises in response to the invitation of the minister. As the meeting continues the lad sits and sobs. An arm goes around his shoulders and a voice says: "My Boy, I'm a stranger to you and to this church, just a traveling salesman, leaving at midnight for the west, but I want to say that the step you have taken you will never regret. I know it from experience, and if you are honestly committing yourself to Jesus He has already received you, and will never leave you. Trust Him, My Boy, all the way. Good-night, God bless you."

He was gone, and the boy out under the stars walking home found the peace that passeth all understanding. For fifty-four years the Jesus Who came into his heart that night has traveled with him. The unknown salesman friend little dreamed of the good he did that night, but God knows, and some day, he who is now a preacher, will see him and thank him.

"Let the redeemed of the Lord say so."

REV. JOHN COMPTON BALL,
Washington, D. C.

"If I ascend up into heaven, thou art there: if I make my bed in hell, behold thou art there."—Psalm 139: 8.

WITHOUT a great faith in God there is no religion. To speak of religion without God is but to attempt to transfer to ethics a dynamic which it can gain only from undergirding by the Divine, whose reality the expression denies. "I believe in God" is the rock upon which religion rests.

But the real eloquence of this passage goes much further. To believe in God is not enough. Religion is cold until faith rises to the SENSE OF THE PRESENCE OF GOD. "The Lord of hosts is with us." Our eyes may see but dimly; but the sensitive soul of the seer lays hold of the vibrant, dynamic PRESENCE "in Whom we live, and move, and have our being," finding HIM everywhere—in the sanctities of heaven, in the loneliness of the grave, in the ends of the universe, and in the very darkness of night. "God is our refuge and strength, a very present help in trouble."

REV. CARL C. RASMUSSEN, D.D.,
Washington, D. C.

"This is the day which the Lord hath made; we will rejoice and be glad in it."—Psalms 118:24.

THE Psalmist probably had in mind a special day, as coming from the hands of God, and he was led to fill it with joy and praise. Should not this be true of all our days, for they all are from the Lord. Life comes to us a day at a time, and I like to think of each one as from the Lord. Any day, every day, today, belongs to Him and is given us to fill up with joy and praise and loving service unto Him. We should let no day pass without being the good Samaritan, or without speaking a good word for our Savior. Each day should be faced with confidence and strength, with joy and hopefulness. It may bring pain and sorrow, trial and temptation, but it will also bring the presence and blessing of Him Who said "As thy days, so shall thy strength be."

REV. CHARLES H. SCHUTT, M.A., B.D.,
Toronto, Ontario, Canada.

"He that heareth my word, and believeth him that sent me, hath eternal life, and cometh not into judgment, but hath passed out of death into life."—John 5: 24. Revised Version.

I AM afraid to die." You are? Then hear the promise of Jesus.

"He"—anyone, "that heareth my word"—receives the Gospel, "and believeth" removes everything that stands between him and a close personal fellowship with Jesus; opens his heart to receive His Spirit; lives every day, everywhere, the principles which Jesus taught, viz., righteousness, love—devotion to the welfare of others, reconciliation, unselfish service, brotherhood—recognizing God as Father, all men as brothers, and the intrinsic value of individual personality, regardless of color, race, or nationality.

"And believeth him that sent me"—believes that "I came forth from God" and that "my teaching is not mine, but his that sent me," "hath"—possesses now, "eternal life"—it does not begin at some future time.

"And cometh not into judgment"—to the believer the judgment is already concluded, for he "hath"—because of his belief, "passed out of death"—separation from God, "into life"—a life lived in personal fellowship with God, begun now and continued after bodily death, through eternity.

Jesus says, "Believest thou this?"

REV. HENRY MOEHLING, JR.,
Philadelphia, Pennsylvania.

"The church in thy house."—Philemon 1: 2.

HAVE you a Church in your house? Do you have religion in your home? You may invest your house with all the adjuncts of comfort, surround it with the restraints of morality, beautify it with the charm of refined education, but if the altar is not found there, if the Book of God's truth is never opened or spoken, if the perfume of prayer is never breathed there, then you do not know the full joy of home life.

No man ever knelt at a higher altar than his mother's knee. No holy light burnt more clear than the flickering firelight at the old home where we bowed in childish faith and lisped our first prayers, and rose with eager glee to receive that blessed kiss from mother's lips as we said "good night." We need the aid of all that Church can offer and the stimulus of public worship and prayer. But we cannot dispense with "the Church in thy house" for the gracious infection of religion is caught in the family circle.

REV. WILLIAM C. SAINSBURY, D.D.,
Fargo, North Dakota.

"I am poor and needy; yet the Lord thinketh upon me."—Psalms 40: 17.

WE ARE poor and needy no matter how rich in worldly goods we are. We have every reason to be very humble before God. We are lacking in strength, wisdom and goodness. The best we can do is to stretch out empty hands toward heaven.

But before we think of God He thinks of us, and His thoughts are thoughts of mercy and truth. His love is the portion of each one of us. If He notices the sparrows that fall, why should it be thought a thing incredible that He should throw around us the wealth of His care? He is our Father, and all our needs are met in Him. How comforting the promise of His abiding thoughtfulness! We may not know the way, but we know our Guide, and that is our sweet support.

REV. CHARLES P. WILES, D.D.,
Philadelphia, Pennsylvania.

"I do always those things that please Him."—John 8: 29.

THIS is uniquely true of Jesus but it may in measure be true of us also, for He is our great exemplar. What an ideal to set before us. In the great faith chapter in the Epistle to the Hebrews we are told that without faith it is impossible to please Him. That statement implies two things: First, that we may live a life that is pleasing to God and in the second place that such a life can only be lived on the principle of faith. The chapter illustrates it for us and cites the names of many in the past who so lived and who were subject to the same limitations as we are. Yet they lived lives pleasing to God. To live such a life we must have Faith in God's word, Faith in the Cross, Faith in His presence, and Faith in His purpose.

Let us trust where we cannot trace and so shall we live a life that is pleasing to God.

REV. DAVID MILLER,
Brooklyn, New York.

"So then let us follow after things which make for peace, and things whereby we may edify one another."—Romans 14: 19.   Revised Edition.

WOULD you make your life a blessing? Then follow after things which make for peace. Think, feel and do what attracts, challenges and enriches others. Through humility, sympathy and love, lead people into wholesome, zestful living. This adds to the sum of happiness.

Peace is more than the absence of discord. It is harmonious, purposeful living. Jesus came from heaven to bring peace. He died bequeathing that peace to us. We live to make it universal.

Such living enriches the world. Peace edifies— builds. It makes possible every kind of progress. Ideals become realities when men provoke to peaceful living. Life responds by doing what expectancy and confidence begets in it, and in the process grows like Him Who is the Prince of Peace.

REV. M. HADWIN FISCHER, PH.D., TH.D.,
Gettysburg, Pennsylvania.

"Beloved, now are we the sons of God."—1 John 3 : 2.

THERE is sonship by nature, being made in the image of God with capacity for dominion. There is sonship by grace, a higher privilege. "Whosoever believeth that Jesus is the Christ is born of God." "Every one that doeth righteousness is born of God." "Every one that loveth is born of God." Believing, doing, loving! The sum of it is,—"To as many as received Him to them gave He power to become the sons of God." Here is faith's great positive, "Now are we the sons of God." And being such, we have a life to live. Sonship by nature, sonship by grace, a great affirmative,—and a life the issue! Being sons of God, set this affirmative in the center of your habitual thinking and daily living. Make it your moral and spiritual rallying cry. The tendency is to become what we imagine ourselves to be. Put into words the privilege of your sonship, and make the thought of it dominant in your life.

REV. CHARLES A. WILSON, D.D.,
Casper, Wyoming.

"And we know that all things work together for good to them that love God, to them who are the called according to his purpose."—Romans 8 : 28.

ALL things? Even affliction and trials and disappointments and failure and loss? Yes, all things. Not all things *are* good, but the all-wise, all-powerful Heavenly Father makes them all work together for good to his children.

Joseph's experiences at the hands of his brothers were not good, but God made them all work together for good.

Paul's thorn in the flesh was not good, but God made it work for good, bringing a new dependence upon God and a new sense of God's power and sustaining grace.

So then just give God His rightful place in your life; seek after and follow His guidance and *know* that whatever comes, "All things work together for good."

REV. HOWARD A GRISWOLD,
Merchantville, New Jersey.

"He maketh his sun to rise on the evil and on the good, and sendeth rain on the just and on the unjust."—Matthew 5: 45.

WHAT a topsy turvy world it seems to be! The evil appear to prosper and the righteous to suffer. The racketeer rolls in wealth while the honest toiler often lacks bread for himself and his family. Is there a God in heaven? Does He care? Jesus met this dilemma but with what assurance. "Sun rise on the evil and good," he said. He not alone admitted it but rejoiced in it. He was glad that the Father's care was over all. The evil do not really prosper. Gangsters kill each other. Injustice brings about its own doom. When we get Jesus' perspective and see things in the light of immortality, we will cease to be envious of evil men. We will catch the meaning of the 83d Psalm. When we learn to trust Jesus' Father as our Heavenly Father we will know that His hand is upon the helm. That assurance will solve our problem. Our Father knows and cares.

REV. WILLIAM HIRAM FOULKES, D.D., LL.D.,
Newark, New Jersey.

"I press toward the mark for the prize."—Philippians 3: 14.

PAUL was perhaps the most outstanding example of Christian perfection since the time of Christ our Savior. But Paul did not regard himself as being perfect. In his own words he called himself "Chief of Sinners." But his one chief desire which possessed his mind continuously was to be more and more like Jesus. At all hazards his aim was to attain Heaven in the end. He was well acquainted with the Athenian racers of his day and how they threw all their strength into the race to win the prize, so he, by the grace of God through Jesus as his ever present Savior must win Heaven. And one of his very last utterances was "I have finished my course. I have kept the faith, henceforth there is laid up for me a crown of righteousness."

Let the same prize be our mark.

REV. WILLIAM H. HARDING,
Cicero, New York.

"Casting all your care upon him; for he careth for you."
—1 Peter 5 : 7.

DEAR Soul, accept this invitation and hand over to God everything that worries and alarms you.

Do you remember the day when you were hurt at play and came running home to Mother? Do you remember how willingly and gently she bandaged the wound, wiped away your tears; and, after holding you close to her loving Mother-heart for a few moments, the pain ceased, the desire to play revived, and away you ran to again take your place in the game? Now, time has made some changes. You, her child grown to manhood, are playing a part today in that larger game called Life. Why is your face lined with care? Where is the old-time smile and sunshine? Yes, cares have come—you have been wounded in the struggle, but have you forgotten your Mother's God? Do you not know that God cares? Now in this quiet moment be a child again. Bend your knees and fold your hands and, in the Name of Jesus, your Savior, cast your cares on God, for He careth for you.

REV. ADAM J. HOLL, D.D.,
Pittsburgh, Pennsylvania.

"Neither pray I for these alone, but for them also which shall believe on me through their word."—John 17: 20.

THERE are two experiences which are very dear to the heart of every Christian. One is the consciousness of the fact that we have some intimate and vital personal contact with Jesus Christ. The other is the spiritual uplift and power which comes from the knowledge that some great and God-like person is praying definitely for us. These two precious experiences are combined in this verse in supreme perfection. What could be more heartening to the devout Christian than the assurance that, on His last night of fellowship with His own, Jesus looked down the centuries and included us in that glorious fellowship? Perhaps only this: that, having been included in that fellowship, we should hear Him say, "I am praying for you."

REV. A. V. CASSELMAN, D.D.,
Reading, Pennsylvania.

"If any man buildeth on the foundation gold, silver, costly stones, wood, hay, stubble———."—1 Corinthians 3: 12, Revised Version.

EVERY Christian has at his hand the materials for building a life to the Master's glory and his own reward. In earthly contests many are handicapped, but for the heavenly prize there is equal opportunity.

Statesman or craftsman, employer or servant, mistress or maid, teacher or student, financier or farmer, alike must find in the daily round the gold and silver and precious stones.

Putting honor into humblest task or largest transaction, playing straight on athletic field or in market place, "giving himself with his gift," whether it be the cup of water or the priceless spikenard, doing the "whatsoever" in the name of the Lord Jesus, so he builds gloriously and imperishably.

"Build thou more stately mansions, O my soul."

REV. C. B. FREEMAN, B.A., D.D.,
Kingston, Ontario, Canada.

"Let every man take heed how he buildeth thereupon."—
1 Corinthians 3 : 10.

A STUDY of "The Seven Deadly Sins" will give some conception of the enemies with which the soul has to contend and "The Seven Cardinal Virtues" will discover great friends the soul may call to its aid. We must build our own life, our character; we must construct the house of man's soul. God calls upon us to make it a "Temple" into which He may come and dwell. This is man's noblest ambition and highest achievement. God's portion is His people and His dwelling-place is not in buildings of brick, stone or marble, but in the hearts of good men and women. There is not much necessity of care when we build one-story houses, but when we are constructing a building twenty, thirty, or fifty stories high, there must be no flaw in line or material. So when we are building a "Temple of God" we must be alert to reject the evil and even more alert and insistent on building in only that which is good.

REV. E. RYERSON YOUNG, B.A.,
Barrie, Ontario, Canada.

"I will now turn aside, and see this great sight."—
Exodus 3: 3.

OUR Father is always trying to get us to the place of spiritual discoveries. Moses beheld the strange fact of a burning bush, blazing, but not consumed. It arrested his attention. God is not interested in getting mere information into our souls; He wants us to have a revelation of Himself. God has challenging futures for us, and will go to miracle lengths to get us to pay attention. What joy of forgiveness and what power of love awaits the listening soul! As "my expectation is for Him" I will listen today. If God calls me from ease and idleness, it will be that His undergirdings are sufficient for a great service. "I *will* turn aside" for it is God who calls me.

REV. WILLIAM BRATTLE OLIVER,
Lynn, Massachusetts.

"But so shall it not be among you."—Mark 10: 43.

AN INSPIRING negative!

The Fellowship of Jesus had been thrown into confusion because two of His outstanding followers sought personal promotion at His Hands. With tender insistence, He called them back, all of them, to a remembrance of the glorious fact that in His Fellowship things weren't like that at all. They must not forget that with Him they were looking at the things unseen and eternal. To be a Christian is to be divinely different. The weights and measurements of the matter-of-fact world are not adequate; only the Stature of Christ now! "It is not so among you."

What redemptive inspiration, what sustaining comfort, what persuasive vision these simple words carry into the heart of the Christian!

REV. IVAN MURRAY ROSE, D.D.,
Philadelphia, Pennsylvania.

"He saved others; himself he cannot save."—Matthew 27: 42.

EVIL seemed to be doing its worst to the innocent victim upon the middle cross. Truth and justice seemed to have left the earth. Yes, truth was upon the scaffold and wrong was upon the throne. Ridicule from priests and scribes and elders charged the ominous air. "He saved others; Himself He cannot save," they said. But they little realized that they were giving utterance to a wonderful prophecy, a profound divine truth. It was just because He came to save others that He could not save Himself. For it was impossible for Himself to be saved from this ordeal if He would save the world, if He would save you and me.

REV. L. FRANKLIN GRUBER, D.D., LL.D.,
Maywood, Illinois.

"The Lord is my shepherd . . . and I will dwell in the house of the Lord for ever."—Psalm 23: 1–6.

THIS is the Psalm of the four "C's." *"Confidence"* in the Lord. *"Contentment"* in the heart. *"Courage"* amidst dangers. *"Completeness"* here, and hereafter.

These are life's four greatest qualities. And they are for us; not for angels! But if we are ever to possess them we must take them in the Psalmist's order.

Confidence in God is first. Contentment can never sing in your heart without confidence. This is true in your home; and among friends. It is true also with God. Nor does courage long live when confidence and contentment are dead. And who could ever hope for completeness in this life, or in any other, without a foundation in God for it?

Let me commend to you the four "C's" of this Shepherd Psalm. Make them yours, and be unafraid. Jesus is the "Good Shepherd."

REV. JOHN GRANT NEWMAN, D.D., LL.D.,
Philadelphia, Pennsylvania.

"And it is my prayer that your love may be more and more rich in knowledge and all manner of insight."—Philippians 1: 9. Moffatt's Rendering.

THE apostle recognized two elements essential to efficient Christian living—Love and Knowledge—heart and head. Some persons abound in love and others in knowledge. Paul would have his followers well poised by the cultivation of both.

Where knowledge is supreme, one may be coldly intellectual; where love is dominating there may be a fervor that lacks judgment. When love is made rich in knowledge, the head and the heart support each other, and intelligence is warmed with love while love is stabilized with knowledge. This means an enriched personality.

In this balanced life one recognizes the things of permanent value—the things that are vital. Life is made beautiful and strong, transparent and fruitful, to the glory and praise of God.

Poise means power energized by the warmth and enthusiasm of the heart and directed by the judgment and knowledge of the head.

REV. GEORGE T. WEBB, D.D.,
Toronto, Ontario, Canada.

"I hate vain thoughts: but thy law do I love."——Psalm 119: 113.

GOD has not only endowed us with the ability to think, but to choose the things we think about. We thank Him for the gift of friends, home and health, but often forget the sanctity and responsibility of this gift which gives us the supremacy over all other creatures.

While it is certain——"As a man thinketh in his heart so is he"——this is also true that——"as he is in his heart, so thinketh he." In it he reveals his power, beauty and loving kindness in the person of Jesus Christ.

In the law of God we can discover what manner of persons we ought to be. We all need its comfort and the inspiration and aid of its precious promises. Trouble, sorrow, reverses and suffering come, but in the Bible we have the assurance that "Underneath are the Everlasting Arms."

REV. JOHN C. BOWERS, D.D.,
Catonsville, Maryland.

"To be spiritually minded is life and peace."—Romans 8: 6.

THE Christian life would prove easier for most of us if only we thought of Christ oftener. If we had a dear friend in China and never gave him a thought, he would even cease to be dear, and presently it would be all one to us as though he were dead. We become like what we think about. We abide in Christ by means of glances of attention fixed upon Him. Thought is the opening through which pour the waters of His great life, to flood the shallows of our nature. To think of Christ is to enjoy His friendship, and can limits be set to what friendship could do for us? No one ever dreamt such dreams for humanity as Jesus did, and we can listen while He speaks about them. Such a companionship in thought will bring us out of ourselves, therefore out of gloom into joy.

REV. H. R. MACKINTOSH, D.D.,
New College, Edinburgh, Scotland

"Come unto me, all ye that labour and are heavy laden,
and I will give you rest."—Matthew 11: 28.

A S FOLLOWERS of Christ we must learn to
take Him at His word. Too often we forfeit
the proffered joy because we lack confidence in
Him. This verse is an offer to relieve us of our
load. The halt, maimed and blind realized the
impossibility of helping themselves and surrendered to Him completely. Without the interfer-
ence of human hearts and minds and with an
acknowledgment of His power He was able to
do the will of God. He Who could restore the
incurable, give back the dead to friends, knows
how to soothe and heal our sorrows when we permit Him to have them as His own.

REV. JAMES F. KELLY,
Wilmington, Delaware.

"For what shall a man be profited, if he shall gain the whole world, and forfeit his life?"—Matthew 16:26. Revised Edition.

WE OURSELVES are worth more than all that we can get. So the Lord asks, "What will a man give in exchange for his life?" and again He says: "A man's life consisteth not in the abundance of the things which he possesseth."

The real problem of life is whether we shall try to make it strong and rich, or permit it to be poor and mean. The richness of it consists in its moral and spiritual quality.

For us, life is interesting only as it involves a striving for goodness against temptations, selfishness, or discouragement and despair. It is the virtue in the world that makes vice attractive to some; and if the world could exist without moral ideals, men would not want it. It would be stale and stupid.

So it is not the army or navy or the material wealth of the country which ensures the stability of the Republic, but the Christian character of the plain people. Therefore Christ says: "Make friends by means of the mammon of unrighteousness," and "Win for yourselves souls."

RT. REV. THOMAS F. GAILOR, D.D.,
Memphis, Tennessee.

"Blessed be the God and Father of our Lord Jesus Christ,
the Father of mercies and God of all comfort; who comforteth us in all our affliction, that we may be able to
comfort them that are in any affliction, through the comfort wherewith we ourselves are comforted of God."—2
Corinthians 1: 3–4.   (A.S.V.)

PERHAPS nothing tests the Christian's faith
so severely as affliction. It is difficult to see
God as the "Father of mercies" in times of sorrow
and trial. Surely, if He were merciful, He would
not allow suffering to come to His child! But
this text shows that affliction is the background
against which God's tenderness is more graciously
displayed. So, in the midst of trial, faith sees
God as "the Father of all mercies," Who comforts
His suffering one, "as one whom his mother comforteth."   (Isaiah 66: 13.)   Through this experience of divine comfort, he is able to comfort
others in the same need.

                    REV. ROBERT MILTON WEBSTER,
                         Germantown, Pennsylvania.

"Joseph is a fruitful bough, even a fruitful bough by a well; whose branches run over the wall:"—Genesis 49: 22.

ONE of the loveliest pictures in all literature, representing what any good man would like to be! The Vine has its roots matted around the garden well. Hence it never ceases growing, even in the most arid summer. So great is its fruitful growth that it pitches its laden branches in, not over the wall. Best of all, by the "law of the road," any weary traveler may find rest under its shade and may pluck of the grapes that hang down into the roadway. Does it not suggest that if our roots are clustered about the wells of God, we too shall grow in fruitfulness and our branches shall be flung over the wall into the roadway to bless and help some poor passerby? It is a beautiful parable of a good man's unconscious blessing.

REV. JAMES M. BLACK, D.D.,
Edinburgh, Scotland.

"Jesus Christ the same yesterday, and today, and forever."—Hebrews 13: 8.

JESUS CHRIST is not like the ever changing fashions, but like the unchanging stars of God. His love is unchanging. His love survived the Cross. His love will never let us go; nor can anyone separate us from his heart. His truth is unchanging. The teaching of Christ can never grow old. He uttered the words of the Almighty and the words of God are eternal. His words were spirit and life.

He is the Savior of yesterday, today, tomorrow. The cross will ever remain the unchanging grounds of forgiveness. The cross is the Power of God unto Salvation. Our changing nature needs this unchanging Christ. If we go to Him, we shall be changed into the image of the unchanging Christ.

"Change and decay in all around I see,
   O Thou, who changest not abide with
      me."

REV. GEORGE MOABA, B.D.,
Philadelphia, Pennsylvania.

"And when he saw their faith."—Luke 5 : 20.

THERE is still a place for faith in this age of law. We have discarded the faith which was a blind leap from the end of reason and have set aside faith as "belief in the things we know aren't so," but faith is constant and eternal if it be founded upon the Rock. The faith of the farmer in the laws of nature, the cowboy in his pinto when they are caught in a blizzard, the faith of a child in his parents when he hears the murmur of their voices as he lies in his little bed. The childlike faith which is in accord with all law and with all observable phenomena still binds man to God and brings the blessing of the Infinite into our lives as in Jesus' day it brought blessing when he saw real faith. Faith is more than hope —it is costly, but it binds man to God.

REV. JAMES W. FIFIELD, JR,
Grand Rapids, Michigan.

"Be clothed with humility."—1 Peter 5:5.

A PLAIN coat is humility. At once we confess our carnal nature dislikes the make and style: pride views it with aversion.

All His earthly life our Lord Jesus Christ wore this artless garment, being meek and lowly in heart, and to the tall tree He carried it, drenching it with His precious blood, when, "he humbled himself—even unto the death of the cross."

An unpopular coat with the crowd; yet One delights to see it worn, "A meek and quiet spirit which is in the sight of God of great price."

Blessed Spirit! Assist us to put on this lowly raiment, for, "humble we must be if to heaven we go, high is the roof there; but the gate is low."

REV. GEORGE DOUGLAS,
Flushing, New York.

"It is for chastening that ye endure."—Hebrews 12 : 7.
Moffatt.

THERE is no Scriptural ground for the prevailing belief that "chastening" means punishment. What a boon it would be if we could
eradicate the idea that suffering is punishment
inflicted by God. We should at once be rid of
much opposition to God. "Chastening" is making chaste, making beautiful, making perfect—
the Spirit's work. What the engraver's tool is to
the precious metal, that is suffering to the precious
soul. By chastening one becomes of more value
to God, to society and to oneself. Jesus was made
perfect through the things that He suffered. This
is not a theoretical view of life. It is strictly
a religious view. No one can accept this view
without trusting God in some sort of way. Nor
can one appreciate this deep saying unless one
has lived deeply. It was by living that the author
of these words found the meaning of living.

REV. A. EDWIN KEIGWIN, D.D., LL.D.,
New York City, New York.

"Who comforteth us in all our tribulation, that we may
be able to comfort them which are in any trouble, by the
comfort wherewith we ourselves are comforted of God."—
2 Corinthians 1: 4.

WHO has not suffered? There are an incredible number and variety of afflictions—of
body, mind, and Spirit.

Here is the source of Comfort—God. But not
a far off God. He is the God and Father with
whom we are joint heirs; Who as the Man of Sorrows, shares all our experiences, suffers all our
temptations, and in the overflowing compassion
of His love, introduces us to the Father. He it
is Who invites us to cast all our care upon Him—
for He cares for us!

In my yard there grows a plant called "Hearts-
ease." But it only releases its rich balsam odor
when it leaves its own soil to rest in the hand
of the one who seeks its fragrance. We are comforted that we may comfort. Lead your friend
to your Father and then you will have not alone
your comfort, but his comfort too.

REV. J. C. MASSEE, D.D., LL.D.,
Boston, Massachusetts.

"A sower went out to sow his seed: and as he sowed, some fell by the way side; . . . and some fell upon a rock; . . . and some fell among thorns; . . . and other fell on good ground, and sprang up, and bare fruit an hundredfold."—Luke 8: 5–8.

THE sower may do his work well, the seed (the Word of God) may be perfect, but the difficulty of receiving the Word is in the soil. How do we receive the Truth? The birds of worldliness steal away the seed before it germinates. Lack of meditation means lack of understanding. "Other" interests, like thorns, choke the Word. Active minds, pure hearts and holy living are absolutely necessary to understand, appreciate and appropriate the saving Truth. Minds that are full of gim-cracks cannot become thoroughly furnished unto good works—make room for Truth by giving Him first place—all the place. We cannot receive more truth until we have lived the truth we now have to the best of our ability. The same SEED that failed to produce in three of the soils produced a hundredfold on the good ground. What a responsibility it is to HEAR: to *receive* His Word; and what a blessing.

REV. H. D. HOOVER, D.D., PH.D., S.T.D.,
Gettysburg, Pennsylvania.

"Thou wilt keep him in perfect peace, whose mind is stayed on Thee: because he trusteth in Thee."—Isaiah 26:3.

CONFIDENCE is one of the Christian's greatest comforts. It assures the mind; it stays the heart; it strengthens the soul. *God is!* The mind believes it; the heart accepts it; the soul is happy in it.

God is good! We are His children! He loves us! This is attested to the believer by the Holy Spirit through the Word of God, and it is verified in his own inner experience by the power of a living faith. *We need God*—His care, His guidance, His deliverance.

All this we have in His Son Christ Jesus, and when we believe His Word and leave all to Him we are kept in the perfect peace which the prophet here portrays.

REV. GEORGE J. GONGAWARE, D.D.,
Charleston, South Carolina.

"Worship the Lord in the beauty of holiness."—Psalm 29: 2.

THREE things I pray that each day He will grant me, so that my soul may grow in beauty until it shall attain holiness: First, that between waking and sleeping I may see something beautiful, not only in the universe that He has made, but in the things that man has created, as well as in human and divine relationships. May His Spirit help me to realize that in seeing beauty, I am seeing Him.

Second, help me not to be satisfied until I have learned the joy of willingly "going the second mile." May His Spirit strengthen me, as I go through life, to do more than is required.

Third, help me to learn something beautiful, and so to make part of my soul the great things in life which He has given for my benefit.

Thus may beauty so color, change and charge my life that I may worship Him in holiness and through His sustaining love may each day realize these three things until I grow to the stature and fullness of my Lord and Savior, Jesus Christ.

REV. HENRY DARLINGTON, D.D.,
New York, New York.

"For I know whom I have believed, and am persuaded that he is able to keep that which I have committed unto him against that day."—2 Timothy 1: 12.

WHAT a triumphant note is in this message to Timothy! Among Paul's converts none was more beautiful in devotion and faithful in comradeship to the Apostle than this native of Lystra. Could any message from Paul have evidenced a more heroic spirit as sent from his prison cell in Rome to cheer the heart of his spiritual companion in Christ? This message to Timothy can be summarized in one word—faith.

This is the dynamic word in the vocabulary of every Christian. The philosophy of rationalism and materialism must not supplant our faith in Him. Belief in the mechanistic theory of creation cannot save us from atheism and agnosticism which are the bane of civilization. But faith in Jesus Christ as the Son of God, will enable us to meet the responsibilities of life courageously and finally triumph with Him as the Redeemer of men. This is our privilege and this is His will.

REV. W. F. TEEL, D.D.,
Reading, Pennsylvania.

"And we know that all things work together for good to them that love God."—Roman 8 : 28.

WE KNOW!" Have you any word in your vocabulary stronger than that? It is pre-eminently a New Testament word. These people you read about in the Acts and the Epistles were people who knew some things and were not afraid to testify, however much their testimony might startle and bewilder people who were without their experiences.

How did Paul and the little group of Disciples in Rome know that? In only one way: by experience. It was not a theory they had accepted, a philosophy of life they had thought out. They had been long enough in this way to be persuaded of the process of which they are speaking. And it was a process, a process in which "all things" —not some things—all things "work together" to produce certain results. *Some* things, standing by themselves, bewilder and terrify. "*All* things work together" in beautiful and orderly harmony "for good!"

REV. WATSON L. PHILLIPS,
New Haven, Connecticut.

"And he that sat upon the throne said, Behold, I make all things new."—Revelation 21:5.

THE great inventions, the new views of life and duty, of brotherhood and service, of universal peace, of the need of banishing poverty, of setting little children free from hard and cruel labor, of giving women the freedom to realize themselves and, by realizing themselves, to make themselves more than ever the servants and the saviors of the race—what does this mean but that God is making all things new. He is making all things new, and He is giving to those who are working with Him, the assurance that their labor will not be in vain. These already see the kingdom of God established upon the earth—a kingdom which fulfills the dream of the saint and seer of Patmos who saw the holy city, new Jerusalem, coming down from God out of heaven. From all eyes God has wiped away all tears. And there was no more death, neither sorrow nor crying, nor any more pain.

REV. WILLIAM E. MCLENNAN, D.D.,
Buffalo, New York.

"If any man willeth to do his will, he shall know of the teaching, whether it be of God, or whether I speak from myself."—John 7: 17. Revised Edition.

IN A time of puzzlement over the tests of spiritual truth and authority, these words of the Master will bear re-emphasis. The final appeal is not to be made to the *intellect,* important as reasonableness is to our normal daily living; nor to the *feelings,* valuable as emotion is for our consciousness of God's presence. The real test is found in being *willing to do* the Father's will. Let a man try the Gospel, and he will discover that it is true. This is no mere glorification of ethical activity, but a hearty, intelligent responsiveness to the challenge to live by the truth that is from Above.

REV. PURD E. DEITZ,
Philadelphia, Pennsylvania.

"He shall not fail nor be discouraged, till he have set judgment in the earth."—Isaiah 42: 4.

THE Savior Whom we trust is the conquering Christ. He knows no discouragement; He anticipates no defeat.

Such was the spirit of His earthly ministry. He never lost hope for His wayward, never wearied in His search for the lost. It was Himself He pictured in the owner who "goeth after that which is lost *until he find it.*"

In this undiscouraged Deliverer is our hope for ourselves and for mankind. Can this life of mine ever become like unto His glorious life? The work is His; He has undertaken, and "He shall not fail." And can this warring, wandering world become indeed a kingdom of God and of His Christ? The promise stands; though the vision tarries we wait and work. *He Shall not Fail!*

REV. ROBERT JOHNSTON, D.D.,
St. Catharines, Ontario, Canada.

"Open thou mine eyes, that I may behold wondrous things out of thy law."—Psalms 119: 18.

THERE are wondrous things in the law of God. The crowning wonder is the revelation of Himself as creator and preserver of the universe, the maker and Redeemer of men, our Savior. And the wonder of wonders is that His amazing mercy and might are brought through His word and works to each individual life in its minutest details for every moment of time.

There is more in the Bible than words and sentences. The luminosity of it is spiritual. The deeper truth in it is the truth as it is in Jesus. The higher goal of it is the redeemed life. The farther reach of it is eternal salvation.

Therefore to see we must see God. He alone can open our eyes to the infinite values of His Word. And to open eyes He can adjust lenses that will magnify the minute and draw nigh the distant wondrous things in His law. Oh, for the seeing eye and the understanding heart!

REV. HIGHT C. MOORE, D.D.,
Nashville, Tennessee.

"Him that cometh to me, I will in no wise cast out."
—John 6:37.

ONLY one man has ever made this statement.
Not the President of the United States, or the
King of England, or the Pope, or any earthly
Potentate ever has or can give utterance to these
words. None other than God Himself could ever
lay such a foundation on which a world of penitent sinners, alarmed souls, desponding believers,
and rejoicing saints may build their hopes and
never be put to shame.

In these few divine words what food for the
hungry soul and peace for the aching heart are
presented absolutely free and certain to "him that
cometh." All men without a single exception have
this blessed assurance of acceptance, if they but
come. It was Mary Magdalene's experience, it
was the experience of the dying penitent thief on
the cross and of Saul of Tarsus. It will be yours,
just as surely as Christ has promised it. COME!
COME TO JESUS NOW!

REV. CHARLES E. KEIM,
Philadelphia, Pennsylvania.

"And said, Verily I say unto you, Except ye be con-
'erted, and become as little children, ye shall not enter into
the kingdom of heaven."—Matthew 18: 3.

UPSTAIRS, in the Sunbeam Class, the little
people gather on Sunday morning. They
raise their baby voices in song, and listen, with
childish wonder, to stories of the Savior. They
are not always quietly devout as older people
are supposed to be in church, nor do they always
grasp the significance of the things that are taught
them; but they love to come to the Sunbeam Class.

We older children will do well to go back to
the Sunbeam Class, when the intricacies of life
become too much for us. The little children know
all that is necessary about God for the salvation
of any life. To them, He is the father of all
life, the maker of the stars and flowers, the friend
and savior of men, and the guide of them that
have gone astray.

Up in the Sunbeam Class there are no creeds,
controversies, definitions, scholarship, sermons;
but there are faith, love, and trust. However wise
we may be we can all learn from little children
that God is love and that the everlasting arms are
about us.

REV. ALVIN E. MAGARY, D.D.,
Brooklyn, New York.

"Now unto him that is able to do exceeding abundantly above all that we ask or think, according to the power that worketh in us."—Ephesians 3: 20.

WHICH is the most precious verse in the Bible?" This is difficult to answer because of our varying moods. In confession, the soul needs cleansing; in sorrow, the heart needs comfort; in perplexity, the mind needs guidance and in these particular needs we want the assurance of pardon, consolation and guidance. When we realize that our Heavenly Father is able to help us in any emergency; that His power is unfailing, His love unceasing, we have assurance that His ability to help is matched by His willingness.

In the above verse we are led to the utmost reach of human thought. Often we falter, many times we fail, sometimes almost despair, then comes the Word, "He is able." We contemplate all that God can do and all that He has promised to do; then everything that we could ask for or think of and still we have not exhausted His resources. What a rich heritage for the child of God; safe in His Father's care; secure from all alarms; he is more than conqueror for "He is able."

REV. CARLTON R. VAN HOOK,
Camden, New Jersey.

"If any man will do his will, he shall know of the doctrine, whether it be of God, or whether I speak of myself."—John 7: 17.

FAITH is a journey. Certainty is its goal. Some get only as far as "I want to believe" or "I'll pretend to believe." Others manage to go on to "I hope" or "I really expect." Many never get to the place where Nicodemus stood when he said, "We know . . ."

How like our modern world it is to demand that we be set down at the goal without making the journey! The doubter says, "Prove to me that Christ is divine, then I'll believe." Do you want to believe? Then live a Christian life. Jesus tells us that if we do God's will, we shall "know of the teaching." It is by obedience to His will that we journey to the goal of a sure faith.

REV. J. H. L. TROUT,
Cleveland, Ohio.

"To the one we are the savour of death unto death; and to the other the savour of life unto life. And who is sufficient for these things?"—2 Corinthians 2:16.

GOD requires faithfulness, not success of His witnesses.

Christ presented in His attractive power, will repel some; others will be reconciled to God. Is man sufficient for this life and death mission? Whatever its reception be, this Gospel will bring forth fruit; such remains an acceptable savor unto God. Our sufficiency is of Him.

We have taken the fifth step in Acts 26:18, "inheritance among them which are sanctified"— God's second gift. No natural qualities will suffice for supernatural ends.

Cato's "Delenda est Carthago" is atheism's insistent slogan, but its demand is the utter destruction of Christianity. We are not in ourselves sufficient to meet this Challenge. Our incapacity will be the only hindrance to the Divine cooperating grade.

"Arise, shine: for your light is come."

REV. M. SCOTT FULTON, M.A., D.D.,
Chatham, Ontario, Canada.

"As thy days, so shall thy strength be."—Deuteronomy 33 : 25.

THERE are times when the duties and responsibilities of life overwhelm us. They rise like dark and forbidding mountains before our minds, so that we are moved to say in our despair, "Who is sufficient for these things?" We need to realize that God requires us to live only one day at a time, and that He promises strength sufficient to perform the duties and bear the burdens that each day brings.

Our Lord told us not to be anxious for the morrow. Most of the things people worry about concern the future and many of them never materialize. Let us take each day as it comes fresh from the hand of God, live life at its highest and best, do the things that seem most important and be confident in this blessed assurance—"As thy days, so shall thy strength be."

REV. CLAUDE O. DIEROLF, S.T.D.,
Philadelphia, Pennsylvania.

"But God commandeth his love toward us, in that, while we were yet sinners, Christ died for us."—Romans 5 : 8.

GOD is not like us. Most errors in thinking today are traceable to a failure to recognize this fact. God is not like us because He is perfect and we are imperfect. He is holy; we are tainted with sin. Perfect hatred of sin must be an attribute of God just as much as is perfect love of the sinner. How then can God hate my sin and love me? You may sweep the realms of human thought but you can never find an answer other than the one that came from God Himself. The cross of Jesus Christ is the perfect solution of this problem. He received the stroke of God's just wrath against sin, and now God's love can flow through to every sinner who will recognize that he has come short of God's perfection and accept the Lord Jesus Christ as his Savior.

REV. DONALD GREY BARNHOUSE,
Philadelphia, Pennsylvania.

"Whose voice then shook the earth . . . that those things which cannot be shaken may remain."—Hebrews 12 : 26, 27.

WE ARE living in a day of testing. Everything is being shaken to its very foundation. During the Great War cities with their magnificent cathedrals and costly buildings were shaken to the earth and reduced to ashes. During this period dynasties founded hundreds of years ago were overthrown. Kings were uncrowned, noblemen of every rank were stripped of their titles and many reduced to actual beggary.

The period of shaking has reached the religious realm. Men are throwing off God altogether. The educated and intellectual classes are rapidly going into some form of unbelief, shutting God and His Word completely out. Witness the teaching of evolution by the professors of Divinity in colleges and the cordial support given to the so-called higher criticism, which when unmasked is infidelity pure and simple.

The world is living in constant apprehension of danger. The child of God even in these days may live with the calm of heaven filling his soul. It will refresh the Christian's heart to be reminded of that. One of the unshakable things is THE THRONE OF GOD. "Thy throne, O God, is forever and ever."

REV. LOUIS T. TALBOT,
Hamilton, Ontario, Canada.

"What doth the Lord require of thee, but to do justly, and to love mercy, and to walk humbly with thy God?"— Micah 6: 8.

THE successful life must conform to divine rules. We must recognize the rights of others and order our actions accordingly. Jesus has plainly stated this in what we know as the Golden Rule.

The motive power of our existence must be love. We must be merciful in our judgment of others for the Master said, "Blessed are the merciful for they shall obtain mercy."

We are known by our friends and our attitude toward them. Let us live realizing that Jesus is nearer than breathing, closer than hands and feet, and humbly striving to please Him Who said, "Ye are my friends if ye do whatsoever I command you." Those who are faithful to the end shall receive the crown of life.

REV. J. E. HARPEL,
Philadelphia, Pennsylvania.

"All things are your's."—1 Corinthians 3: 21.

ALL things at all times can be used by all men for soul-making. In this sense all things are ours. Because teachers differ, we are forced to do our own studying, thinking and praying, and so we achieve convictions which are really our own. Some say that nature is foe, some that she is indifferent, others that she is friend. One thing is certain, she can be used. Nature can teach us the glory of beauty, the value of order, the wisdom of humility before the unimaginable immensities of time and space, and also the wisdom of submission to the inevitable. Life, all of it, the bright and the dark, is ours and so is the certainty of death. There is nothing in the present; there will be nothing in the future that will not work out for good. "All things are yours: and ye are Christ's; and Christ is God's."

REV. HENRY A. VRUWINK,
Albany, New York.

"A voice came out of the cloud, saying, This is my beloved Son: hear him."—Mark 9: 7.

THERE will be many calls to each of us today.
Some will be answered through love, duty or
necessity.

Let us hear a new call and respond for a different reason. It is the Father who says, "Hear
ye Him." In the confusion about us let us heed.
When He sends us into the business of living
today, the struggle may make our need of Him
very real. His word to us is "I am with thee."

Our supreme kingdom service may be at hand.
Remember His "So send I you."

We may walk in our own or in another's
shadows. Will not this help us then? "No man
shall pluck them out of my Father's hand."

REV. ED C. COFER,
Portland, Oregon.

"The Lord shall preserve thy going out and thy coming in, from this time forth, and even for evermore."—Psalms 121: 8.

THESE words shine like stars. Each new day, let us take them for our horoscope, discovering in them the good fortune which awaits us.

Who? "The Lord"—of love, light and life.

What? "Shall preserve thee"—as shepherds protect their sheep, as fathers guard their children from the crush of despondency, the infection of sorrow and the dominion of sin.

Where? "Thy going out and thy coming in." He will keep us as we go out in the morning to labor, and come home at night to rest; as we go out in youth to begin life, and as we come home at eventide to die.

When? "From this time forth and even for evermore." Under the protection of this promise, we may live each day without fear or dread.

REV. J. GORDON JONES, B.A., B.TH.,
Toronto, Ontario, Canada.

"Acquaint now thyself with him, and be at peace."—
Job 22:21.

ACQUAINTANCE—literally "Companionship"
—results from knowledge of, communion with
and obedience to God.

The heathen worship nature's phenomena in
fear. The Bible reveals God as Creator, and
Nature loses its dread. Nature seen through God's
Word becomes an expression of a Father's love
for His children.

We *know* people by hearing of and corres-
ponding with them, or reading their writings. To
be *acquainted* with people is to talk with them,
exchange confidences, know their motives. So
with God. Communion (prayer) is talking *with*
God. But God also talks with us. He reveals His
desires if we will listen. That is communion.

Obedience,—it results from *knowledge of* and
communion with God. "*Blessed* is the man that
walketh not in the counsel of the ungodly . . .
But his delight is in the law of the Lord" (1st
Psalm 1 and 2 verses). "Thou wilt keep him in
perfect peace whose mind is stayed on Thee."

REV. ROBERT R. LITTELL, D.D.,
Philadelphia, Pennsylvania.

"He sent his word, and healed them."—Psalms 107: 20.

AT NO time in the history of the world has the consciousness of truth been so needed as in this day and age. The masses and classes are enveloped in a fog, pitifully attempting to grope their way out. The eternal message of a resurrected Christ has been lost sight of—and yet there it stands like a beacon, flashing its gleam of Hope. Health is His gift to the universe. The Holy Bible is a treasury of inspired healing thought, a demonstrable fact in human existence.

The Great Physician who never prescribed drugs for anyone, or gave the slightest attention to man-made theories, is the Way, the Truth and the Life. He can save us from sin, deliver us from sickness, annihilate the fear of death and enable the whosoever will that may come, to drink at the fountain of living waters. "Ho, everyone that thirsteth, come . . . without money, and without price."

REV. THOMAS J. NOONAN,
New York City, New York.

"From the days of John, the Baptist, until now the Kingdom of Heaven suffereth violence, and the violent take it by force."—Matthew 11: 12.

THIS word of Christ upsets those who think His discipleship a peaceful pursuit of happiness. Under His leadership there never can be a truce with the forces of evil nor a compromise with sin; nor any doubt of the final outcome—complete victory. He permitted His enemies to crucify Him only in order to undo their own purpose. His glorious resurrection sealed their doom, but also aroused them to still more determined though futile violence against His followers. "The blood of martyrs is the seed of the Church," remains true to the end of time. Why then be fearful? The violent, *i.e.* the energetic, determined, fearless in His Name face the consequences, conquer self and enter the Kingdom of Heaven by force.

REV. E. F. BACHMANN, D.D.,
Philadelphia, Pennsylvania.

"God . . . hath shined in our hearts, to give the light of the knowledge of the glory of God in the face of Jesus Christ."—2 Corinthians 4: 6.

HOW beautifully *intimate:* in the face of Jesus Christ. Paul had not actually seen that face; nor can *we,* save as Paul came to see it— in the deep experience of fellowship with Him.

It is hard to know God—increasingly difficult in days when so many problems have become persistent: faith in a *personal* God, everywhere active in this immense universe; faith in a *loving* God, despite the fact of evil; faith in *moral imperatives* as coming *on divine authority.*

We make God real through Jesus Christ, Who translated God into terms of human life and expressed God's thought in human speech.

Not merely, Christ is God-like; but God is Christ-like. What Christ was, God is; all that He said, felt, did, God says, feels, and does.

RT. REV. CHARLES FISKE, D.D.,
Utica, New York.

"Thou wilt keep him in perfect peace, whose mind is stayed on thee: because he trusteth in thee."—Isaiah 26:3.

SPIRITUAL poise, so much needed in the stress of modern life, is not a human achievement; it is a gift of God. God has not simply created our mental machinery; our thoughts are His present care. We are not to cultivate calmness, we are to cultivate God. This sacred intimacy of the soul realized, the great result ensues. "The peace of God shall guard your hearts and your thoughts in Christ Jesus."

The word "peace" is suggestive of the process. In the Greek, the thought is adjustment after alienation. An alien is one who owes allegiance to another country. The secret of our modern unrest is that men, living in God's world, are still owing allegiance to some other sovereign. They are not right with God, and so nothing is right.

REV. ALEXANDER MACCOLL, D.D.,
Philadelphia, Pennsylvania.

"At that time Jesus answered and said, I thank thee, O Father, . . . for so it seemed good in thy sight."—Matthew 11: 25, 26.

A VISITOR to a school for the deaf and dumb wrote on the blackboard—"Why has God made me to hear and speak, and not you?" The little ones sat dazed before that dreadful "Why?" A little girl arose. Her eyes were swimming with tears. Walking to the board, she wrote—"Even so, Father, for so it seemed good in thy sight."

How precious it is to believe that He doeth all things well, that He knows, cares, chooses and that we are not children of circumstances but children of an infinite, loving Heavenly Father through faith in Jesus Christ.

"Simply trusting every day,
    Trusting through a stormy way,
Even when my faith is small,
    Trusting Jesus, that is all."

REV. ALLEN S. WHEATCROFT,
Philadelphia, Pennsylvania.

"But love your enemies, and do them good, and lend, never despairing."—Luke 6: 35. Revised Version.

IT DOES not say "never discouraged," "never perplexed," "never disheartened," "never sorrow nor grieve," but "never despair." The Bible overlooks no situations in life yet its constant message is never despair. The most assuring passages and triumphant songs came to men in their deepest and most trying hours; against the midnight background a light steadily burns. Surely Jesus had much cause to despair, He came down the years with the storm in His face and on the night when going out to face the hurricane of Gethsemane and Calvary said to His disciples, "Let not your heart be troubled, trust in God." His message was trust God against all odds or appearances.

Despair is the hand that pulls down the shade refusing to let God's sunshine in, the anarchist that would drive God out of His universe. Let us never despair of the goodness, wisdom, or providence of God.

REV. JAMES MILLAR,
Twin Falls, Idaho.

"For we have not an high priest which cannot be touched with the feeling of our infirmities; but was in all points tempted like as we are, yet without sin."—Hebrews 4: 15.

THERE are no words of "Holy Writ" so full of comfort and consolation for weak and frail humanity as these words which tell of the sympathy and compassion of Jesus. The heart of humanity yearns for sympathy, for some one who can enter into the sorrows and trials of life. We are told in this passage that Jesus is such a one. He knows our frailties, our straits and troubles, outward and inward. They are not hid from Him. There is no pang of grief that wrings any human bosom but sends an answering thrill through the loving, pitying heart of Jesus, Who intercedes for us at God's right hand. His sympathy is no less remarkable than His love. It is the essential qualification for His office of High Priest.

Whatever the experience may be there is something in the heart of Jesus that responds to it. Let us be encouraged with the thought that Jesus knows and cares.

REV. ELIJAH J. GREGG, D.D.,
Jacksonville, Florida.

"I came that they may have life, and may have it abundantly."—John 10: 10.   Revised Version.

THUS Jesus expressed His purpose as He found His fellowmen hampered by disease and poverty, bound by chains of evil habit and sin, walled in by narrow prejudice, dense ignorance and silly superstition, and kept from beauty and joy by innumerable fears. Knowing to what heights of character man could rise and believing that every personality created in the spiritual image of God was of limitless value, He went about liberating the bodies, minds, and souls of men. A cross on a lonely hill could not stop Him. In His name we may share the joyous, though arduous, campaign against the slavery of ignorance, injustice, sin, and fear. In partnership with Him we may know life at its fullest, freest and best.

REV. FREDERICK L. GILSON,
Missoula, Montana.

"Every one therefore who shall confess me before men, him will I also confess before my Father which is in heaven."—Matthew 10: 32.   Revised Version.

THIS word of Christ has come down the ages with unsullied clearness; and its attractive vitality is as powerful as ever. Whether regarded as a promise to His faithful people, or as embodying a definite undertaking on His part in the eternal interest of those who call Him Lord, it is a word upon which the believer may implicitly rely. The message is this:—Those who confess Christ before men, serving Him in the life of the world, will in due time be confessed by the Son before the Father and the holy angels. Why not "lean hard" upon this plain assurance? The followers of Christ are destined to be the peculiar treasure of their Lord in the "crowning day."

REV. JAMES W. THIRTLE, LL.D., D.D.,
London, England.

"I beseech you therefore, brethren, by the mercies of God, that ye present your bodies a living sacrifice, holy, acceptable unto God, which is your reasonable service."— Romans 12: 1.

OUR body is the finest, noblest house we have in this life, we are besought "By the mercies of God," such as His grace, the gospel of Christ which is the power of God unto salvation to every one that believes, and eternal life, to present our body, not dead but a living sacrifice, holy, with assurance this is acceptable to God.

The person dwelling in this body is to be transferred by renewal of mind, into the image of Christ, using God's word and sacraments and other heavenly things as pure words, honesty, truthfulness; love, helpfulness, kindness; peace, uprightness, pure living; so by faith united with Christ and each other, our world becomes better and to us is assurance of joy and eternal life.

REV. JOSEPH O. GLENN, B.S., A.B.,
Wheeling, West Virginia.

"Casting all your care upon him; for he careth for you."
—1 Peter 5: 7.

CHRISTIANS too frequently are victims of fear. They walk in an atmosphere of tragedy. An indefinable evil presence stalks beside them. Must we merely bear it? If there is no relief, of what use is our Christianity? Peter bids us cast our anxieties and fears upon God the Father. A thousand years before the birth of Christ the Psalmist said, "Cast thy burden upon the Lord, and He shall sustain thee."

To do just that is our definite duty and privilege. Only as we realize our limitations can we understand the power and loving kindness of the Father. Most of our burdens are heavy but not real.

We are heirs of the promise "He careth for you." Patriarchs, prophets and Jesus tell us that God loves and cares for us. A cloud of witnesses of the past twenty centuries give the same evidence. As we believe their testimony we find Peace.

REV. HARRY BURTON BOYD, D.D., LL.D.,
Philadelphia, Pennsylvania.

"If ye shall ask any thing in my name, I will do it."—
John 14: 14.

IF OVER our church or our life the word
"Ichabod" may be written it is because we
have failed to heed this verse. Every promise has
one end wrapped around the throne of God and
is interwoven with His very integrity. His Word
cannot be broken. If one promise should fail it
would shake the very foundations of His throne.

Are we conscious of weakness when temptation
assails the citadel of our soul, or under the burdens that oppress us, or in carrying out the task
committed to us? Are our lives barren spiritually
and does sorrow crush us with its pall of grief?
Across all the need of our life and all the un-
satisfied longings of our souls may be written the
words of James, "Ye have not, because ye ask
not!"

REV. A. GORDON MACLENNAN, D.D.,
Pittsburgh, Pennsylvania.

"Which we have as an anchor of the soul, a hope both sure and stedfast and entering into that which is within the veil."—Hebrews 6: 19. Revised Version.

W E MAY admire the ship's anchor, chained to the bow of the vessel, and feel a sense of security in seeing it there; but it is only when the anchor is cast into the sea, and has disappeared from view, that it fulfills its office as an anchor. Then we know that we have an anchor, not because we see it, but because our ship is steadied by it.

So with the Christian's "anchor of hope." It is of value when cast within the veil, within the "secret place of the Most High." Then are we conscious of its presence because we are steadied by it. In the unseen anchor we have confidence; and we realize that our lives are hid with Christ in God.

REV. DE WITT M. BENHAM, D.D., PH.D..
Baltimore, Maryland.

"Let us therefore come boldly unto the throne of grace, that we may obtain mercy, and find grace to help in time of need."—Hebrews 4: 16.

THE free and open access to God is life's greatest privilege. Sin robbed us of the privilege, but the new and living way to God has been opene for us through the death and resurrection of our Savior, the Lord Jesus Christ. We may come boldly to the throne of grace, when we come in His name and plead His merits. Under all circumstances we may come and make our desires known to God. When we come, we will meet the great High Priest Who is touched by our infirmities, because He was tempted in all things like we are. In His name we can come, and have the assurance that we will find mercy and help in the time of need. Therefore let us come!

REV. G. E. WALLENDORF,
Kenosha, Wisconsin.

"Who is on the Lord's side?"——Exodus 32: 26.

SOME Christian people came to Abraham Lincoln in the darkest days of the Civil War and said to him, "We trust that the Lord is on our side." The reply of Lincoln was, "I am not so much concerned whether the Lord is on our side as I am that we should be on the Lord's side."

Is the Lord on our side? That is not important. Are we on the Lord's side? That is all important.

Our side may be the right side and it may be the wrong side. It may have justice and it may have truth with it and it may not. The Lord's side is the side of right and justice and truth. Our first duty is to find out what side the Lord is on and then align ourselves with that side. Then find something to do and do it. Get to work.

REV. HEZEKIAH L. PYLE, D.D.,
Riverhead, Long Island.

"Let the redeemed of the Lord say so."—Psalm 107: 2.

DON'T talk about doctrines or theories. Share your actual experiences of religion with others. Suppose you have discovered that it is vitally worth while to go regularly to church because it serves to remind you at least once a week of certain attitudes toward God, your fellow men and yourself that otherwise you might easily forget. Then out of your actual experience, speak to your friends. Suppose you have discovered that with all the complexity of life in our generation you can keep yourself calm and steady and effective and purposeful by setting aside some time each day for solitude, when, in quiet, you think about all the things you are doing in the light of God's purpose for you and for the world. Then, out of your actual experience, speak to your friends. This is better than all religious argument. "Let the redeemed of the Lord say so."

REV. T. GUTHRIE SPEERS,
Baltimore, Maryland.

"Trust in the Lord with all thine heart; and lean not unto thine own understanding. In all thy ways acknowledge him, and he shall direct thy paths."—Proverbs 3: 5, 6

A FATHER and his small son, while waiting for a train in a strange city, started to walk hand in hand, down the main street and away from the depot. Realizing that the lad did not know where the street was leading, the father said to him, "Where are you going, my boy?" Without hesitation and with perfect assurance, the lad replied, "I do not know, but you do." He was not concerned about the way so long as his father was his guide.

We are strangers in a strange land. We do not always know where our path is leading. Like the lad, if left to our own understanding, we would not know how to find our way. But we can have the assurance that our heavenly Father will direct our steps and bring us home at last, if we put our hand in His by trusting Him with all our hearts and acknowledging Him in all our ways.

REV. PETER W. SNYDER, D.D.,
Pittsburgh, Pennsylvania

"Thy faith hath saved thee; go in peace."—Luke 7:50.

JESUS is the guest of a Pharisee. A woman enters the guest room. She performs a courtesy which puts to shame the host. Jesus recognizes it as an expression of faith. Hence: "Thy faith hath saved thee; go in peace."

It is always an honor to have Jesus as a Guest in your home. His presence always brings a blessing. He recognizes and accepts every expression of love and devotion. He never spurns the expression of repentance from the worst sinner. "Though your sins be as scarlet, they shall be whiter than snow." Every life is precious in His sight. No sin is too great for His forgiveness. He is willing to enter any kind of home. Yea—He stands at the door and knocks. Open the door of your heart and home. Let Him enter!

REV. J. MAURER, D.D.,
Kitchener, Ontario, Canada.

"To the church in thy house."—Philemon 1 : 2.

PHILEMON'S house was the church in Colosse. There he conducted worship for his family and the neighbors. It was not just a common house. It was the house of God.

Can we make our home a "Church in thy house?" Every Jewish home was a house of worship. The Lord's Supper was instituted in a private house, a simple, family meal. The Holy Spirit fell on the disciples in the upper room of a private home.

There is need for organized religion on a large scale. But that cannot take the place of home religion. One is the big spring rain. The other brings daily showers of refreshment.

We must perfume the atmosphere of our home with the Word of God, the voice of prayer, the songs of Zion, quiet moments of meditation, like this one. Then all common tasks shall be glorified, and all life shall be holy unto the Lord.

REV. WILLIAM OSGOOD ROGERS, D.D.,
Denver, Colorado.

"For I am not ashamed of the Gospel of Christ: for it is the power of God unto salvation, to every one that believeth."——Romans 1: 16.

ABIDE with Jesus and with His precious Gospel because it is the only thing which will make you happy, truly happy both in this life and in the world to come. The Gospel is the glad tidings of the grace of God. As long as you sincerely believe in the Saviour Jesus, you will find that the Gospel is truly the power of God unto your salvation. It will assure you that it was for your sins also that Jesus died on the cross, that, though you remain sinners as long as you live, your transgressions have all been blotted out. God is pleased with you for His Son's sake, and that nothing can happen to you against the will of God. And when death comes and you must leave this world, the Gospel will enable you to face the last grim foe without fear and trembling. You will commend your soul into God's hand and depart in peace, falling asleep in Jesus.

REV. B. WALTHER PFEIL,
Hudson, New York.

"Surely the Lord is in this place; and I knew it not."—
Genesis 28 : 16.

JACOB had got mixed up in some very ugly
transactions and, fleeing from the wrath of his
brother, he was tired from the day's journey and
he fell asleep. He awoke, amazed to find God
was with him in mercy and kindness, hence the
exclamation! The common tendency is to forget
that God is always with us, although Jesus said
it very definitely. Our daily transactions would
be different if we could bring ourselves to the
realization of this fact. On the other hand, what
comfort there would be amid our disappointments
and sorrows. In every one of us is a sanctuary
which God never leaves. "Know ye not that your
body is a temple of the Holy Spirit which is in
you, which you have from God?"

REV. PETER AINSLIE, D.D.,
Baltimore, Maryland.

"Be still, and know that I am God."—Psalm 46:10

MOST of us have interpreted this verse as an incentive to quietness and meditation before God, but the Hebrew word signifies more than this. The only time this particular word is used is in the Old Testament. The derivative means an exactness—"Take a slack in the rope," in other words. It is not simply an admonition to be quiet, but to let the tension go out of our life, just as the great cable holds in place the great steamer until the vessel reaches its channel and can go with its own steam.

So we are to wait before God and take a slack in the rope—just let the tension go. It is Paul's thought, when he wrote to the Philippians, "Be anxious for nothing."

Such a confidence and trust in God will take the wrinkles from the brow and lead to that "Peace of God which passeth all understanding."

REV. JOHN TIMOTHY STONE, D.D.,
Chicago, Illinois.

"The just shall live by faith."—Habakkuk 2: 4.

THESE mighty monosyllables have changed history. They suggest opened windows, battered-in doors, breaking chains, and the glad cry of emancipated souls. It is only the man or woman of faith who really lives. We must make the irreligious man see that the man of faith can beat him in living, beat him not in the tinselled rewards of life but in its quality, its range, its experiences, in all that goes to make life.

The just do live. Faith is not accepting frustration, it is insuring fruition. It is not sacrificing the present for the future, it is taking both the present and the future. Faith is not depleting life, it is completing life. Faith is rejecting poison and accepting life, for to be carnally minded is death but to be spiritually minded is life. Faith belongs not in the obituary column but in the birth list. Through faith we come to the discovery of a great God for ourselves, to the achieving of a Christlike character in ourselves, to the merging of a great cause with ourselves. The just shall live.

REV. FREDERICK BROWN HARRIS, D.D.,
Washington, D. C.

"Be of good cheer; I have overcome the world."—John 16: 33.

TWO prison walls confine us: the physical body and the material world. From this circumstance arise all fears.

Jesus said, "Fear not!" This word carries divine power to the believer. Living beyond all fear gives us poise in salvation.

It can be done, for Jesus, as Christ, "overcame the world." He vanquished the material order. By faith we can "think and will" in Him, as Paul said, "I can do all things in him . . ."

Christ functions in love. But love casts out fear, as it discerns, in all earthly experiences, the spiritual challenge and espouses it.

What can harm us if we constrain what seems materially dreadful to yield us spiritual and eternal benefit? Our Lord converted His material cross into a sign of spiritual victory. "Therefore will we not fear, though the earth be removed."

REV. JOHN R. BROYER, PH.D.,
San Francisco, California.

"By this shall all men know that ye are my disciples, if ye have love one to another."—John 13: 35.

THE world is concerned largely about commercial and industrial problems. The struggle for existence has grown worse in this complex age. Man in his desire for food, housing, and clothing has at times lost sense of the moral law and with his physical demands has sacrificed ideals. Christ, in His day, recognized such a condition in the world and He trained His followers to rise above the level of this life. Love was to be paramount. His disciples were not merely to teach love but they were to show it in their actions. Christianity was to be a living force in the affairs of men. He gave the membership of the church a task when He charged His followers with a new precept, "Love your enemies." A sign of a true Christian is not what he believes but how he shows his discipleship. This old world would revert to the law of the jungle if it were not for the men and the women who hold fast to the faith of their fathers and apply that faith and love in the solution of the problems of life.

REV. CHARLES HENRY LONG,
Philadelphia, Pennsylvania.

"I am come that they might have life, and that they might have it more abundantly."—John 10: 10.

WHAT a breath-taking truth! *"I have come"* —just another way of saying, "Before Abraham was, I am." All others began to be; our Lord is pre-temporal, definitely coming out of the eternities for a definite purpose. Then too, the *quality* of life He gives. *"That they may have life"*—not just physical, intellectual, moral, nor even a vague kind of spiritual life; but life alive and deep with eternal meaning here and now—a present-tense reality throbbing in the soul. "And this is life eternal, that they should know Thee, the only true God, and Him Who Thou didst send, even Jesus Christ." Moreover, this quality of life the Biologist from Eternity gives increases in *quantity* forever. . . . *"Abundantly."*

REV. FREDERICK F. SHANNON, D.D.,
Chicago, Illinois.

"And said, Verily I say unto you, Except ye be converted, and become as little children, ye shall not enter into the kingdom of heaven."—Matthew 18: 3.

HE IS wistful and wondering, with questions in endless flow; and teachable, it is enough that "Mother told me" or "Daddy says so." He is frank—if he doesn't like you, you will be duly informed—and eager, hopeful, expectant. He is joyous, smiles come even through tears; his sky is blue, his year always at the spring, and everything makes music for him. He is trustful—no one wishes him ill, no one will injure him, all are his friends; the night's bad dream is driven out if Mother is near, and he will go anywhere unafraid if he can find his father's hand.

Are there those who seek the highest seats in the Kingdom? The very entrance is barred except they become as this little child. "Second childhood," with its suggestion of senility, is a phrase transformed by the word of Jesus and thereby opens to us a field of life rich in loveliness, honor and power.

REV. WILLIAM HERMAN HOPKINS, D.D.,
Albany, New York.

"But what are they among so many?"—John, 6:9.

THE account of the miraculous feeding of the five thousand with five loaves and two small fishes is full of counsel and instruction.

Life is always showing us our inadequate supplies. We are tempted to reason our way through our difficulties. We forget, as the disciples did, that what we have on hand, added to what God can supply, will always prove sufficient.

The little you have on hand is all that God expects you to contribute before the process of Divine multiplication begins. In the midst of life's trials and perplexities, there is one sure thing we can do. We can believe in the Providence of God and in His immediate and personal activity.

Let us also learn to do what God tells us to do. Obedience to Law—obedience to God unlocks for us the resources of Omnipotence.

REV. FRANK M. URICH, D.D.,
Philadelphia, Pennsylvania.

"My Grace is sufficient for thee."—2 Corinthians 12 : 9.

THE prayer of a man of faith unanswered! The thorn in the flesh not removed! A servant of God allowed to be buffeted by a messenger of Satan!

The Defeat of Prayer? The crushing of religion? No! The victory of the soul. The prayer which is not answered as men count answers to prayer is answered in a larger and more glorious way. Not the direct bestowal of the gift that is craved, but the gift of those spiritual allies which raise a man's soul to a higher level and make him victor and not victim. "My grace . . . sufficient for thee." The thorn remains in the flesh, but there is a new song of victory upon the lips. "Most gladly therefore will I glory in mine infirmities, that the power of Christ may rest upon me, . . . for when I am weak then I am strong." The meaning of our religion is not to be counted in terms of gratification of our desires, but in terms of the victory of our souls. It comes to us not to remove our thorns in the flesh but to give to us "grace sufficient."

REV. HARRY F. BAUGHMAN,
Philadelphia, Pennsylvania.

"Neither is there salvation in any other, for there is none other name under heaven given among men, whereby we must be saved."—Acts 4: 12.

IF YOU acknowledge the saving power of Jesus Christ, the Son of God, you have nothing to do but to disconnect your affections from the world, place your hopes and desires in heaven, devote your lives to God, leave all your cares with Him, and "rejoice evermore." Praise and joy and trust are the best returns you can make to God for all His love. Fulfill your duty to Him, and He will fulfill His promise to you. Give Him no cause to distrust you, and you need never distrust Him. Take Him for your all, and He will be all to you. He will be your Father, your Friend, your Savior, your Protector, your Support while here, and your everlasting portion beyond the grave.

REV. WILLIAM A. E. SCHEWE,
Wilkes-Barre, Pennsylvania.

"He could not be hid."—Mark 7: 24.

A REAL worth and value cannot be hid. Character shines forth. So the virtue of Jesus, His purity, conviction of heart, He could not be hid.

Those who met Him, loved Him, because of His evidence of wisdom, love, power, these fruit forth. Such a life cannot hide. Because of His appearance, life within, effects life without. Virtue writes its history on the physical, so does sin. Art has done its best to picture the physical Jesus. His eyes, voice, the whole physical Jesus appealed to the people—even to little children.

He is not hidden: He just lives and affects the life possessing the life of Jesus. It is revealed in the personal life, the life of home and community. When a man attempts to hide his religion, he has none to hide. There are no silent partners in the Kingdom of Christ.

REV. HARRY E. WIEAND, D.D., PH.D.
Lancaster, Pennsylvania.

"He that dwelleth in the secret place of the most High shall abide under the shadow of the Almighty."—Psalm 91: 1.

HERE is a direct promise made to the humble child of God that carries with it proximity to the heavenly Father far beyond our most ambitious dreams. Deliverance from every kind of danger; refuge under the pinions of His sheltering wings; freedom from cares and anxieties that bring disquiet to the soul; relief from fears and doubts that shackle the mind; guardian angels doing sentry duty while Father and child hold sacred converse.

The price? Yes, there is a cost attached to such rare privileges. But the cost may be met in a medium of exchange such as the lowliest can easily pay. The promise is to him "that dwelleth in the secret place." Wonder of wonders, can it be true?

The "secret place," my friend, may be established in any home, or even place of business. It is the prayer closet.

REV. C. M. BRITTAIN, D.D.,
Jacksonville, Florida.

"In thy presence is fulness of joy."—Psalm 16:11.

RELIGION is normal. It is not something apart from life, it is life. It is larger than any human interpretation of it. It cannot be encompassed within the content of any definition. It cannot be identified with any place, or ceremony, or ritual seeking to express it. It belongs to no age, but to all the ages. It stoops to help the lowest, yet forever transcends the highest. It meets man at the point of his need, and makes him adequate against any foe that humanity is heir to. It is a thrilling, ending quest for reality, truth and moral grandeur, in all personal and human relationships. It is the reconstruction of individual life, into such an adjustment to the will and purposes of God, as will enable Him to lift life to its noblest possibilities. There is no experience, common to life, but that the musings of the Eternal Mind murmur about us; there is no spot in this boundless universe, but there the attuned soul may hear the eternal soliloquies of God.

REV. WALTER EDWIN GUNBY, D.D.,
Newark, Delaware.

"He had yet one, a beloved son: he sent him last unto them."—Mark 12: 6. Revised Version.

THIS verse tells a fascinating story of the uttermost love of our Heavenly Father.

He gave all! Nothing is withheld. He emptied Himself of His last and dearest holding. He drained the cup—an exhaustion of divine giving. It was the extremity—not the second mile but the last step. There was no reservation of divine grace—no withholding of eternal love. It was the last!

"Immortal Love, forever full,
Forever flowing free.
Forever shared, forever whole,
A never ebbing sea."

REV. BREWSTER ADAMS,
Reno, Nevada.

"And we know that all things work together for good to them that love God, to them who are the called according to his purpose."—Romans 8:28.

IT WOULD seem almost the essence of irony, certainly as a merely foolish play upon words, and yet to me this passage has always carried the conviction of the impossibility of any real disappointment, anywhere in the Universe, for any Divinely-obedient and Divinely-ordered life. A disappointment ordinarily implies the failure or defeat of an expectation, hope, wish, desire, or intention, and to be a real disappointment it must be a miscarriage, failure, or defeat that interferes seriously, permanently, or irreparably with the purpose and possibilities of life. Can there be such a thing in any properly-directed, properly-regulated Christian life? Have we not permitted ourselves to be imposed upon? To be unnecessarily burdened and saddened? May not what we call "disappointments" be but the Divine indications that we must travel another road? Or make up the sum of life in some other way?

REV. ROBERT C. MILLIKEN, B.D., D.D.,
Ottawa, Ontario, Canada.

"Fear not: for I have redeemed thee, I have called thee
by thy name; thou art mine."—Isaiah 43: 1.

EARS as well as lips are necessary to make
a message effective. The Heavenly Father is
ever speaking to mankind; ever voicing anew his
promise; ever enriching them with his overflowing love; ever assuring his children that they are
known by name. Those who listen may hear His
still small voice at morning, noon, or night and
be both comforted and strengthened.

Haste is never helpful to meditation. "Be
still, and know that I am God," suggests the way
to a better acquaintance with the Most High, and
the assuring word "Fear not: thou art mine."

Silence opens the heart's door to heavenly vis-
itants, in whose presence love, joy, peace, long
suffering, gentleness, goodness and faith, come to
fruitage, and beautify the life.

RT. REV. FREDERICK T. KEENEY,
Atlanta, Georgia.

"And he said, Of a truth I say unto you, that this poor widow hath cast in more than they all."—Luke 21: 3.

HOW love magnifies things! The widow's mites were only one-fourth of an American penny but her love magnified the gift a million times. Where love is, the gift is enlarged. Loveless giving means a meager beneficence. Love does not look at the dollar mark, it sees only the Cross of Christ. Love makes the gift bigger in God's sight.

Love magnifies all service. Without love service is slavery. How easy it is to serve those we love. True service and hatred cannot live together. Out of His love the Master gave himself for us.

All living is glorified when the heart is full of love. Where love reigns every duty is precious, every relationship is hallowed, and life glows with heavenly radiancy. To really love, what a difference it makes!

REV. P. D. BROWN, D.D.,
Columbia, South Carolina.

"The Spirit also helpeth our infirmity: for we know not how to pray as we ought; but the Spirit himself maketh intercession for us with groanings which cannot be uttered. . . . And we know that to them that love God all things work together for good."—Romans 8: 26, 28. Revised Version.

IN THE dark hours of trial which come in every life, the human heart needs help and comfort. There are times, such as sickness and death, when even our dearest earthly friends have no power to cheer us. Then do we feel our utter sense of loneliness, of feebleness, and inability to help ourselves.

These are the times when we can only find peace and comfort feeding our souls upon God's holy word, and pleading His promises at the mercy-seat. Here we bring our wounded hearts, for earth has no sorrow that Heaven cannot heal. At such times our text has been a bright pole-star to guide many a storm-tossed soul toward the heaven of rest. It is a message which sparkles out in the blackness of earth's gloom like a diamond in the sky, but it beckons and woos and guides us to a home beyond the skies.

REV. GRAYSON Z. STUP, B.D.,
Harrisburg, Pennsylvania.

"Let your light so shine before men that they may see your good works, and glorify your Father which is in heaven."—Matt. 5 : 16.

COMMON speech is one of the miracles of divine providence. How marvelous that my words may direct your thoughts! But the language of a life is even more eloquent and effective. It is sure of a reading. "Christians are the world's Bibles." It is spontaneously sincere. It is a universal language;—all can understand. Years after David Livingstone lived among them the untutored native of Africa said, "Yes, we knew Jesus; he lived among us." It is a language that every man *can* speak. There is a general timidity with Christians to testify by public speech. Some are without the advantage of education, may even be illiterate. But there is an unmistakable simplicity in life-words; their meaning is apparent. No matter who I am or what is my station, I may by my good works lead men to glorify God.

REV. HENRY ANSTADT, D.D.,
Chambersburg, Pennsylvania.

"And the night following, the Lord stood by him, and said, Be of good cheer, Paul: for as thou hast testified of me in Jerusalem, so must thou bear witness also at Rome."—Acts 23: 11

GOD does not have to be in a hurry. The night following our trial will answer His purpose. Elijah gave Baal first chance, and Abraham gave Lot first choice, and waited until God came. Exemption from trial is not promised, but His presence in the trial is promised. The Lord stood by him, and assured him of the attainment of life's highest and best aspirations.

The realization of our best aspirations may be attended by unfavorable and untoward conditions. But it is also true, that whatsoever God has promised, that will He fulfill, unfavorable and untoward conditions to the contrary notwithstanding. Take courage, fearful and troubled heart. God will not violate an antecedent promise. He will be with us in the crisis of life.

REV. FLEMON SANDERS,
Commerce, Texas.

When I call to remembrance the unfeigned faith that is in thee, which first dwelt in thy grandmother Lois, and in thy mother Eunice; and I am persuaded that in thee also."—2 Timothy 1:5.

A YOUNG minister, lonesome, homesick, and discouraged, made a pastoral call. The lady said to him, "You do not know me. I used to be Miss ...., and now I am Mrs. S......... I knew you when you were a boy. I hope and pray that God will use you greatly and make you a successful minister. You had a wonderful Mother. She was the best woman I ever knew. She helped me and has been an inspiration to my life. God bless you."

The young minister was thrilled to the very depths of his being. The next Sabbath he was conscious of a new spiritual power. He had new joy in the pulpit and as he preached, he intuitively felt his Mother was praying for him.

REV. CALVIN G. BUTLER,
Kansas City, Kansas.

"I am an ambassador."——Ephesians 6:20.

A COUNTRY sends an ambassador to another country to promote good will between his own country and the one to which he is sent.

When an ambassador stirs up ill will his usefulness is at an end.

When St. Paul wrote these words he did not mean that he was the official representative of his country but of Christ. He was commissioned to promote good will between men and women of the world and God. We who call ourselves Christians have a similar commission. We have been commissioned to tell men and women that He wants to bring about a Brotherhood of Man in God.

By unlovely dispositions, by selfish living, by all unChristlike conduct, we defeat the purpose for which we were commissioned. For the time being we are out of commission.

REV. WEBSTER WARDELL JENNINGS,
San Francisco, California.

"And the greatest of these is love."—1 Corinthians 13 : 13. Revised Version.

THE day has passed when a man is truly independent. One writer has illustrated this very vividly, "When he rises, a sponge is placed in his hand by a Pacific Islander, a cake of soap by a Frenchman, a rough towel by a Turk. His merino underwear he takes from the hand of a Spaniard, his linen from a Belfast manufacturer, his outer garments from a British weaver, his shoes from a Brazilian grazier. At breakfast his orange is served by a Florida negro—his coffee is poured by natives of Java and Arabia and his rolls provided by a Kansas farmer."

From this evident physical inter-dependence man has evolved the idea of "Tolerance." But tolerance is not enough. Mere tolerance we resent.

Beneath the color of our complexions there are human hearts and God-given souls which cry out for love—not only tolerance. Jesus touched one of the deepest needs of man when He said—"A New Commandment I give you—that ye love one another."

REV. CHARLES TREXLER, D.D.,
New York, New York.

"In your prayers make intercession for all men."—1 Timothy 2 : 1.

HOW thankful we should be to our gracious Lord and Master, that by His own inspired Word every believing Christian has the high privilege and the sacred duty of intercession. No angel in heaven has any privilege so exalted as to come into His immediate presence and intercede. Only once a year did even the High Priest, in Old Testament days, dare to come into the Holy of Holies to make his annual intercession for the people, and then not without blood. Yet we whose greater privilege it is to live in the Gospel era, dare to come and ought to come, into His immediate presence to make intercession for our fellowmen, not once a year, or once a month, or even once a week, but every day of our life, by the blood of Jesus, His own eternal Son, the divine Savior of all the world.

REV. CHARLES L. FRY, D.D.,
Germantown, Philadelphia, Pa.

"The former treatise . . . of all that Jesus *began* both to do and teach."—Acts 1: 1.

JESUS *began*—doing certain things in His life-time:

He *continued*—working in the lives of His followers.

All the leaders of the early church were constantly aware of his unfailing presence and this knowledge made them different people. The world very soon saw the difference, for other people were quickly changed likewise.

The ineffective, futile lives of Christian people today have often been the cause of much comment and concern. Might we not become contagiously effective, even as they were, if we too were only aware of His Presence?

The city's lanes may be filthy,
The lives of men sordid and mean;
When the Master walks through, with me
or with you,
They are radiant, and happy, and clean.

REV. ROBERT HARRIS GEARHART, JR.,
Philadelphia, Pennsylvania.

". . . wash me, and I shall be whiter than snow."
—Psalm 51: 7.

WE WOULD proclaim that nothing could be whiter than snow, but under a powerful microscope the apparently pure-white snow flake contains many imperfections. By Divine inspiration the Psalmist exclaimed: ". . . wash me, and I shall be whiter than snow." Matthew says that the resurrection angel was clothed in "raiment white as snow." He speaks of the garments of Jesus in the transfiguration scene as "white as the light." John visualizes some inhabitants of heaven and speaks of them as "clothed in fine linen, white and clean." Some standing around the throne are thus arrayed: "What are these which are arrayed in white robes? These are they which . . . have washed their robes and made them white in the blood of the Lamb." Heaven demands white robes. All the signboards on the highway of heaven say: "Keep thyself unspotted from the world."

REV. MARVIN R. GUICE,
North Long Branch, N. J.

"This is my beloved Son, in whom I am well pleased; hear ye him."—Matthew 17:5.

THE world about us was never more disturbed about the person and the authority of Jesus of Nazareth than it is today. It never chafed more under the insisting of conscience that He be heard. And it is also true that the world was never more at a loss to account for the failures in life; the broken marriage bond; the shattered home; the wreckage of every prospect for an honorable, successful life, in spirit of education, wealth and political influence, than it is today.

It is impossible to believe that God, our Maker, ever meant it to be so. It has become so in spite of a gracious, bountiful, good, God. All has come from wrong thinking—wrong living. Here, in the midst of it all is God, the Father's remedy: "This is my beloved Son, in whom I am well pleased; hear ye Him." And here is the Master's modest appeal: "Take my yoke upon you, and learn of Me." This is God's Message for you and for me. If we heed, life's mysteries will become solved problems instead.

REV. SAMUEL J. McDOWELL,
Baltimore, Maryland.

"Be clothed with humility."—1 Peter 5 : 5.

THERE is a proper way for Christians to dress. Peter had learned that by a painful experience. He had gone in for recognitions—what we would call badges of preferment. Then, when he stood at the head of the Twelve, he had denied his Lord. "And Jesus looked on Peter," and Peter remembered that Jesus had taken a towel and girded Himself and washed His disciples' feet. Peter was converted. Never again did he think first of himself. If his Lord thought first of service and wore a servant's towel, Peter would clothe himself with humility. He would wear the Christlike robe of service. He would be remembered by his clothes, but they should be the clothes of a servant.

REV. HERBERT C. ALLEMAN, D.D.,
Gettysburg, Pennsylvania.

"Praying . . . for all saints . . . and for me."—Ephesians 6: 18, 19.

PAUL said, "Pray for me." He was a theologian. Theologians have a peculiar work to do that no one else can do. They train university and college graduates for the Christian ministry. They have a great responsibility. They need our prayers. Paul was a missionary. Home and foreign missionaries are counting upon the people in the home churches to intercede for them. As we pray, souls are saved. Barriers are removed. Darkness is dispersed. Missionaries are strengthened. God's will is done.

Paul was a preacher. We need to pray for the preachers. Pray that they might have physical strength. Their vigor is reflected by the attention or inattention of the audience. Preachers are tempted to compromise. The ecclesiastical atmosphere is pregnant with the spirit of pussyfooting. If you would have the minister speak as he ought to speak, *pray for him!*

REV. ROY TALMAGE BRUMBAUGH, D.D.,
Tacoma, Washington.

"Have not I commanded thee? Be strong and of good courage; be not afraid, neither be thou dismayed; for the Lord thy God is with thee whithersoever thou goest." —Joshua 1: 9.

THESE words were addressed directly by Jehova to Joshua as he stood face to face with the greatest crisis of his career. Having been for many years Moses' minister, he was now called to be his successor as the leader of the Children of Israel. In the face of such a responsibility, it was natural that he should hesitate.

But being assured that he had the approval of the Lord of Hosts and of the promised Presence, all sense of fear, weakness and dismay disappeared. He entered courageously and wholeheartedly upon his trying task of leading a disheartened people into the Land of Promise, attaining a degree of success that even Moses had not accomplished. "If God be for us, who can be against us?" "I can do all things through Him that strengtheneth me."

REV. JAMES CLEMENT REID, PH.D., San Francisco, California.

"If ye then being evil, know how to give good gifts unto your children; how much more shall your heavenly Father give the Holy Spirit to them that ask him?"—Luke 11: 13.

THERE are so many things that we want, that we seem to need desperately, and He passes them by and says that a new spirit is the greatest gift any man could receive. As the years have gone by and I have seen more of what makes happiness, and constructive expenditure of time and energy, I have begun to understand that if we can be freed from fear alone, not to mention all the other desires, that we have just exactly what we really want and really need.

When we have God's spirit, which is the spirit of love, there comes a release from fear, a quiet feeling of power. With this comes a smoother working mind and a gentler but firmer disposition. We are released within ourselves, we grow. We have more vision and at the same time more common sense. It brings a harmony within us and makes us far more effective in our life's occupation, whatever it may be.

REV. JAMES MADISON STIFLER, D.D.,
Evanston, Illinois

"Verily I say unto you, Inasmuch as ye did it not to one of the least of these, ye did it not to me."—Matthew 25:45.

LIKE our Master we must go about doing good. But we dare not forget that invariably He made temporal interest a means to spiritual ends. So we must give the words of today's lesson a spiritual interpretation. That is, we must feed the spiritually hungry, give drink to the spiritually thirsty, clothe the spiritually naked, visit those who are spiritually sick and in prison. This may apply to individuals, societies, organizations, and corporations. And while we are doing all this it must constantly be remembered that we are not saved by our virtues or good works. The best of these are but filthy rags in the sight of a holy and righteous God. "By the works of the law is no man justified."

REV. URBAN C. GUTELIUS,
Philadelphia, Pennsylvania.

"And he answering said unto him, Lord, let it alone this year also, till I shall dig about it, and dung it: and if it bear fruit, well; but if not, then after that thou shalt cut it down."——Luke 13: 8, 9.

FOR three years the fig tree had produced no fruit. The owner decided to cut it down because of its fruitlessness and its absorption of the moisture and sunshine which the vine should have had.

The vinedresser pleads for one more chance for the tree; just one year more of digging and fertilizing. Then if no fruits appear he too will agree to its destruction.

Today, the Parable applies to all who have enjoyed Christian benefits and yet have produced so few fruits of Christian living. It is also a challenge to all who have done but little for the Master to do much for him. The "One more year" is left to us to produce the abundant fruits of the Christian life before we stand at the Judgment Seat of God.

REV. SETH N. GENUNG,
Troy, New York.

"Be careful for nothing; but in everything by prayer and supplication, with thanksgiving, let your requests be made known unto God."—Philippians 4: 6.

ONE of the most precious texts in God's Word for me is found in Philippians 4: 6-7, "Be careful for nothing; but in everytning by prayer and supplication, with thanksgiving, let your requests be made known unto God. And the peace of God, which passeth all understanding, shall keep your hearts and minds through Christ Jesus." This has been my "year text," and it proved such a marvelous source of help, comfort, encouragement and sustaining strength, that I shall use it again. God has kept His promise contained in this passage, and beyond doubt He will continue to do so. Try it. You will not be disappointed.

REV. HOWARD AGNEW JOHNSTON,
Milwaukee, Wisconsin.

"But seek ye first the kingdom of God, and His righteousness; and all of these things shall be added unto you."
—Matthew 6:33.

EVERYTHING in this world that is worthy of possession costs effort. Only those who seek, find. The pebble by the wayside does not seek, and remains a pebble forevermore. The acorn cast into the ground sends out its tender rootlets and gathers in the substance and moisture of the soil and becomes a hale green tree and stands for a hundred years in all its glory. None of us have measured up to all that we might have been if from our earliest activity we had given our services unreservedly to the advancement of God's kingdom.

The seasons of the year follow in direct order, one after the other. The numerous stars are rushing at a speed that no man can know, yet there are no accidents in the skies. Would it not appear strange if God should have an order for the seasons and the stars, yet should forget to have an order for the souls of men? God did not forget and he urges that we seek first His kingdom.

REV. CAMERON HARMON,
Lebanon, Illinois.

"As his part is that goeth down to the battle, so shall his part be that tarrieth by the stuff: they shall part alike."—1 Samuel 30: 24.

THIS is David's ultimatum to certain evil-minded men who would have withheld from others what was their due. It is so easy to recognize the services which are rendered in the public eye. It is so hard to do justice to those who labor quietly, unselfishly, unobtrusively. And yet in the creation of our civilization, it is the men and women who have labored faithfully, persistently, and self-sacrificingly, yet inconspicuously, who have played the greater part. Christian character is but the incarnation in a human personality of the divinely approved virtues, motives, and ideals, and thus the bringing heaven down to earth.

The greatest contribution a human being can make to his day is the living of a life, however humble and obscure, which will introduce into the society some of the gifts God most wishes men to have.

REV. LEWIS S. MUDGE, D.D., LL.D.,
Philadelphia, Pennsylvania.

"For the Word of God is living, and active."—Hebrews 4 : 12. Revised Version.

THE Word of God is "LIVING." It is not a mere outward form, not a dead letter. It has properties possessed by no human word. It is instinct with the life of its divine source, from which it is never divorced. Its promises can never fail, its threatenings never prove idle. It has within itself a living, quickening, life-communicating force.

What a precious message this "LIVING WORD" brings to the devout soul! It quickens faith, inspires to service, and brings comfort. It is the soul's true spiritual food, containing Christ, the Divine Manna from heaven, and he that eateth of that bread shall never hunger. By making daily, faithful use of this "LIVING WORD," our Spiritual life will increase, grow and expand into healthful and fruitful vigor.

REV. JEROME M. GUSS, D.D.,
Phœnixville, Pennsylvania.

"I have yet many things to say unto you, but ye cannot bear them now."—John 16: 12.

THE revelation of divine truth waits on our capacity to receive it. There is a large part of the Bible which can only be understood by us when we come to the place for which the words were intended. "In the time of trouble He shall hide me in His Pavilion" means nothing when the sun shines, and we are without a care or a trial. Those words are reserved for those in trouble. "My grace is sufficient for thee" means nothing to those with no sense of need. But when one has prayed for the removal of a "thorn in the flesh," and it still persists, such words reveal new sources of strength. This is the law of the divine revealing. We learn the truths of God as fast as we are able to take them in and appreciate them, and we may be sure no time will come without its appropriate light, strength, or solace.

REV. HARRY J. NEWTON,
New Haven, Connecticut.

"Like as a *father* pitieth his children."—Psalm 103: 13.
"As one whom his *mother* comforteth,"—Isaiah 66: 13.

THE father and mother love of God are for us who have been born into His Family by the new birth. For us the loving pity of a father and the sympathetic comfort of a mother go out in infinite yearning as He sees our foolish and futile attempts at self-help. So He lets hardship, tribulation, suffering slip through the aperture of His permission, that we may be driven back on His almightiness and love. Our darkest hours become thus our widest doors into the Father's heart, for the child in trouble and tears is ever the one who best finds the meaning and tenderness of a mother's love. Thus also, through the very suffering our foolish hearts would choose to avoid, our Father finds His finest opportunity to show an unbelieving world what His character, lived out in His surrendered children, is like. It is only when the geranium leaf is sadly bruised that it fills the air with the sweetness of its delicious aroma.

REV. J. E. CONANT, D.D.,
Chicago, Illinois.

"If ye shall ask anything in my name, I will do it."
—John 14: 14.

THIS is the Master's promise of loving care for His redeemed. When days are dark and dreary and thou callest unto Him for light, lo, the darkness recedes and He lighteth thy way. When burdens press and thou art crushed beneath life's load, He comes and underneath thy burden He puts His everlasting arms and lifts the galling load from thy heart. When sorrow breaks the spirit and melts the eyes to tears and he soul cries out for relief and peace, He comes and in tender, loving words whispers, "Let not thy heart be troubled, neither let it be afraid," "Lo, I am with thee alway."

REV. CHARLES E. LIEBEGOTT,
Akron, Ohio

"I am the vine, ye are the branches: He that abideth in me, and I in him, the same bringeth forth much fruit: for without me ye can do nothing."—John, 15:5

THE little tendril of the vine is frightened, worried, troubled beyond measure. How can it ever keep its moisture and its life away up there on the hottest part of the trellis? It is small, weak, helpless. Far from the ground, it is the prey to the winds, alone and undefended. So it worries and distresses itself, a slave to its fears. Till the great Vine through whose veins slowly pulses the sap of life, whose roots even on the hottest day are deep in the cool earth, whose life is warm within it even on the bleakest night of winter, answers to the frightened little tendril:—"I am the Vine, ye are the branches.

"Anything you can do by yourself is infinitely small, but it is infinitely important that you keep one with Me. He that loveth Me abideth in Me."

PRES. JOHN EDGAR PARK, D.D., LL.D.,
Norton, Massachusetts.

"This is the way, walk ye in it."—Isaiah 30:21.

IT IS easy to get on the wrong road; but we must watch and pray that we choose the right path and continue thereon. Our daily prayer should be for grace and guidance that we keep on the King's Highway.

Blessed Lord, we earnestly pray that Thou wilt help us to walk with Thee, day by day, on the way of faith, love and duty.

We should ever "Remember Jesus Christ," so that by the charm of His life, the power of His example, the dynamic of His words, the compassion of His heart, and the fidelity of His ministry, we may be inspired, not only to enter upon the heavenly way, but to continue thereon unto the end of our pilgrim journey.

"Keep Thou my way, O Lord, myself I cannot
    guide;
Nor dare I trust my erring steps one moment
    from Thy side;
I cannot think aright unless inspired by Thee;
My heart would fail without Thy Aid; choose
    Thou my thoughts for me."

REV. JOSEPH F. HARTMAN, D.D.,
New York City, New York.

"We love him, because he first loved us."—1 John 4: 19.

G OD is love," and "herein was the love of God manifested in our case, that God hath sent his only begotten Son into the world that we might live through him."

When we know and believe this wondrous truth, the basal fact of the gospel of redeeming grace, we have the witness of the Spirit that we are the children of God. We love Him, because He first loved us: and this ever-deepening love enriches our knowledge of God and things divine; it purifies us by expelling from our hearts the lusts of the carnal man and by molding us into the likeness of its object; it makes us find in the service of our fellowmen that obedience to the Father's will which is the true freedom and blessedness of eternal life.

REV. FREDERICK W. LOETSCHER, D.D., LL.D.,
Princeton, New Jersey.

"Watch ye, stand fast in the faith, quit you like men be strong."—1 Corinthians 16: 13.

WHAT God needs is strong men to do His work in the world, not only men strong in muscle, but men of spiritual power. Paul suggests that a strong man is the alert man. Another characteristic of a strong man is faith. "Stand fast in the faith." A man of faith is one who is steadfast in the great principles of truth that have come to him as a Christian. Another characteristic of a strong Christian is gameness. "Quit ye like men." Don't you hear Paul saying in the language of the baseball game or football game, "Be a game sport! Don't complain." If you are knocked down in the game of life, get up again, rub the sand out of your eyes, and go ahead with a smile on your face and win the victory that is yet to come.

REV. HOWELL S. FOSTER,
East Falls, Pennsylvania.

"And Enoch walked with God."—Genesis 5:24.

TO WALK with God is an incomparable privilege. It should be man's highest ambition. A life wholly dominated by the will of God should become the believer's supreme quest. There is nothing above or beyond this. It opens the way to the best there is at the end of the journey, and all along the way the believer's spiritual treasures are protected, safeguarded, and increased. Victory over temptation is certain. The meaning of life is made clear. Human relationships are sanctified, the commonplace is glorified, and future felicity is assured.

It may involve the giving up of some things which are among our most cherished earthly possessions. Indeed it may send us to the school of suffering and sacrifice. It does call for an unconditional acceptance of the divine program. But this is not too high a price to pay for the privilege of *walking with God.*

REV. FOSTER U. GIFT, D.D.,
Baltimore, Maryland.

"And my speech and my preaching was not with enticing words of man's wisdom, but in demonstration of the Spirit and of power."—1 Corinthians 2: 4.

DEMONSTRATE," what a word! It is great to "demonstrate" how to cook a good meal, build a house, raise a crop, or catch a basket of trout. But to "demonstrate" the "Spirit of Christ," ah, there's a real challenge.

Any craven intellect can put his words into fine phrases, but to incorporate "His Spirit" in our life, to "demonstrate" it! To "demonstrate" it when tired, harassed, upset, betrayed, misunderstood, not in words of wisdom, but in the "Spirit and Power of God."

Too many times we know not this Power. And herein is our hope. To "demonstrate" is hard, but we are to do it, not in our own strength, but in the "Power of God."

When we incorporate His Spirit into our lives, breathe that Spirit, then to "demonstrate" will be easy, automatic, and natural.

REV. CHARLES G. COLE, A.B., S.T.D., *Butte, Montana.*

"He shall cover thee with His feathers, and under His wings shalt thou trust: his truth shall be thy shield and buckler. Thou shalt not be afraid."—Psalm 91: 4, 5.

ALWAYS to fear the Lord and never be afraid, that is the ideal which God has for us. The two are joined with strong fastenings. During the war a son who had been under sharp fire comforted his parents in this country with this, "It is not where you are, but who is looking after you." If we could only get rid of the terror that surrounds so many of us. "Peace and safety." We find them in Him. Living in constant dread is no way for a child of God. Soft, gentle protection and strong, unbreakable defense. Why be afraid while protected against the subtle evils that creep in silently or the evils that make bold attack?

Start each day with this assurance of perfect protection guaranteed in His many exceeding precious promises which never fail.

Rev. W. Courtland Robinson, D.D.,
Philadelphia, Pennsylvania.

"I am come that they might have life, and that they might have it more abundantly."—John 10: 10.

ARE we trying to travel along the path to God, pausing here and there for some Christian deed, with a philosophy of life in one hand and an ethical system in the other?

When we arrive in the presence of God, He will search us for holiness. No system of ethics was ever conducive to holiness. Holiness is the essence of the Christian life. We cannot have an incentive to holiness without the Life of Him who came to give us life abundantly. No philosophy of life can bring forth results acceptable to God, apart from the life of Christ.

Christianity is a life possessed, the life of the Incarnate Word.

A man to be a Christian must understand the fundamental truth of Christ—to be in Him and to have Him in us.

RT. REV. HARRY S. LONGLEY, D.D.,
Davenport, Iowa.

"But they that wait upon the Lord shall renew their strength; they shall mount up with wings as eagles; they shall run, and not be weary; and they shall walk, and not faint."—Isaiah 40: 31.

THIS glorious promise is mine. How I need it every day! My ability to meet the pressure of duty, the unexpected sorrow and the sudden attack of sin is so feeble—so fleeting. My impatience to rush into each day's duties, so often, has revealed the absence of a protecting armor; my feet were unshod and my hand held no sword. My strength was but the strength of man.

This glorious promise offers me a precious privilege of His Holy Presence. Here I may contemplate His Fatherhood—His sacrificial Saviorhood. Bow in humble, happy worship, O my soul, before your Father, your Savior and your constant Companion! In His Presence are joy and peace—also, admonition and commission. "Come—wait" gives place to "Go—serve." Now I may rise and radiate the power of His Presence through loving service—yea, even through trying, difficult service, in the program of this day of grace. Waiting upon Him gives me the strength of His comradeship for every duty and disappointment of life.

REV. WILLIAM C. NEY,
Upper Darby, Pennsylvania

The Master Key: "What lack I yet?"—Matthew 19:20.

IN THE group following Jesus in Judea there was a young man who asked the way of Salvation. But when Jesus told him, the young man said: "all these things have I kept—what lack I yet?" Then Jesus told him what his lack was and "he went away sorrowing." The interview was over, Jesus had asked for the Master Key and the young man refused to give it.

Has Jesus the keys to your life? Has He the key to the library of your life, or do you just read what you please? Has He the key to the dining room of your life, or don't you feed your soul by prayer? Has He the key to the recreation compartment, or do you just go where you please? Have you given Christ the Master Key to your life?

REV. RICHARD H. JONES,
Atglen, Pennsylvania.

"Be still, and know that I am God."—Psalm 46: 10.

HOW aften have we thought and said, "I have so much to do I do not know how I will ever get it all done?" But then have we analyzed what we have to do and why we have to do it? Our present life plays many pranks on us. Often we are like that Old Testament soldier, "so busy here and there" maintaining and extending our own popularity and influence that we, too, neglect larger duties and responsibilities to ourselves and to our fellowmen.

The world greatly needs to draw aside and just "Be still, and know that I am God."

Know that He who made all things and who gives life to all things, still is our God. The Defender, Comforter, Helper, and Redeemer of His faithful children.

REV. THEODORE S. REES,
Winnipeg, Manitoba, Canada.

"Sir, we would see Jesus."—John 12:21.

CURIOSITY may have moved these Greeks, and may move us. More marvels surround His name now than then. "The pre-eminence," was Paul's phrase. Among the colossal figures of history Jesus has the pre-eminence. We would learn why.

Religious feeling may draw us. A scientist wrote lately of the "sense of sacredness" which belongs to man. Another greater scientist writes: "The most beautiful thing we may experience is the mystic and mysterious." And Jesus is the greatest religious teacher this world has known,— among seers, saints and sages the chiefest, the One altogether lovely.

Seeking faith joins curiosity and religious inquiry. Not as scientists would we see Jesus; but as sinners; not as reasoners, but as believers.

> "Then into His hand went mine;
> And into my heart came He;
> And I walk in a light divine,
> The path I had feared to see."

REV. O. C. S. WALLACE, D.D., LITT.D.,
Baltimore, Maryland.

"Other seed fell on good ground."—Luke 8:8.

MANY things go wrong in life, like the seed in thorny and stony soil. But we should not let that make us cynical. Remember that some of the seed went right! There is plenty of friendly soil for the will of God to live in. Today let us make it a business to talk of the good things that are going on. There are lots of good people in this world. There is plenty of fidelity, more than matching the infidelity that is advertised in the courts. There is plenty of love and grace and beauty, in spite of all the devilment that is displayed in the headlines of the daily press. God is not dead nor His will defeated!

REV. J. HENRY HARMS, D.D.,
Philadelphia, Pennsylvania.

"Built upon the foundation of the apostles and prophets, Jesus Christ being the chief corner-stone."—Ephesians 2: 20.

THE Apostle Paul had a statesmanlike program. With superb strategy he would move from city to city, capturing each in turn for his Lord. He would not stop even at Rome; he would go to the farthest bounds of the Empire, to Spain. But when he reached Rome, he was forced to stay. He was laid aside as a prisoner. For God has His own strategy, too. Here the Apostle wrote those great Epistles. Kept from winning the Empire, he was used by God to win—the world!

From a prison-house Paul spoke of God's supreme purpose to bless—to give His children a *character*, pure, holy, loving; a *citizenship* without unneighborliness; a *church* that is missionary; and the *Christ*, sacrificial and supreme.

Our text shows Jesus Christ as "Foundation—Sacrifice." God by his great Foundation—Sacrifice would bless us and build Christ's life into the Church.

REV. EDMUND H. OLIVER, PH.D.,
Saskatoon, Saskatchewan, Canada.

"Lo, I am with you alway."——Matthew 28:20.

THIS is a definite promise of our Lord to us if we really love Him and obey His great command. To have Jesus with us is life's greatest joy. He changes everything. His presence is the secret of our power. Troubled hearts are calmed, fears are banished, and doubts are dispelled. Tasks that once seemed impossible are now accomplished, and our ideals are raised to attempt greater things. Even our worst temptations are overcome when we walk with Him; and our greatest sorrows, when His light is cast upon them, become the entrance into the larger life. When our souls are fearful as they are tossed on Life's seas, it is wonderful to hear Him say, "Be of good cheer; it is I; be not afraid," and then to go forward constantly hearing Him say, "Lo, I am with you alway."

REV. WILLIAM J. MILLER, JR., D.D.,
Philadelphia, Pennsylvania.

"What think ye of Christ?"—Matthew 22 : 42.

TO THINK one must have experience. If one has not had the experience of study or personal observation there is not much room for thinking. When we come to religion most of us have had certain experiences. At some time or other we must all face the question of the text.

It ought to be a great joy to every Christian to know that Christ is God manifest in the flesh. That He is your Savior and mine. That He died in our stead and for our sins. By His obedience and suffering He redeemed us.

Do you think of Him as your personal Savior? Do you feel that you need Him daily? Have you ever thought that all you are and have is due to Christianity? When you receive Him as your Lord and Savior then you can really enjoy Him in true fellowship of the spirit.

REV. A. C. KANZINGER,
Ardmore, Pennsylvania.

"We know that all things work together for good to them that love God."—Romans 8:28.

GOD knows what is good for us better than we do ourselves and will make all things work together for our good if we love Him. *"We know* that all things work together for good,"—that is the expression of a conviction born of experience.

It is *all things* that work together for good: sickness and health, defeat and victory, adversity and prosperity, the blossom that matures into luscious fruit and the flower that turns to ashes in our hands—all things!

All things *work together.* They work together as salt and sugar work together to make food palatable; as various ingredients in a medicine work together for the restoration of health; as sunshine and shower work together to ripen harvests.

"To them that love God": that is the clincher! We need not fret and fume about how things will come out; but we do need to be careful that we love God. It is an active ethical passion, a sovereign principle of life. We must keep step with God's commandments against all the forces that oppose us, and fulfill Christ's summary of the law: to love God with all heart, soul, strength and mind, and our neighbors as ourselves. When we love God, we know that all things work together for our good.

PRESIDENT DANIEL L. MARSH, LL.D.,
Boston, Massachusetts.

"In my Father's house are many mansions: if it were not so, I would have told you."—John 14:2.

THE word "mansion" suggests a house of large proportions. What Jesus really said was, "In my Father's house there are many abiding places." The very word which we use for "home" in this world indicates how temporary it is. We speak of it as a "dwelling." A dwelling is a place where we delay—linger—tarry, all reflecting the transitoriness of this existence. But in the Father's house there are many "abiding places." That means permanency, security, rest and peace. Then Jesus adds: "If it were not so, I would have told you." Jesus was clear and honest in all of His teachings. Would Jesus have led men to believe in a life beyond, if there were no such life? We can rest with full believing assurance on this; "In the Father's house there are many abiding places!" else Jesus would have told us.

REV. MARCUS E. LINDSAY, D.D.,
Wichita, Kansas.

"Acquaint now thyself with him, and be at peace; thereby good shall come unto thee."—Job 22:21.

DEEP down in the soul of man there is a yearning for God. "Thou hast made us for Thyself and our soul is restless till it rest in Thee" is still the echo of man's deepest need.

Acquaintance comes through knowledge. We find God in His Word. We find Him in human experience. To know God is to love Him. We can talk with Him and read his messages of love. *Now*—today—is the invitation of the text.

Jesus knew the Father and went to Him for comfort and strength. Peace of mind, tranquility of soul and spiritual power flowed back from those moments of meditation. We, too, may have the same comfort and strength today, if we will "chum" with God.

REV. JAMES FISHER, A.B., B.D.,
Phoenix, Arizona.

"Behold we go up to Jerusalem."—Luke 18: 31.

THIS gospel presents a journey—a last journey and full of world significance. There
must be no retreat—no disaster, no broken hope.

In 1812 Napoleon invaded Russia with 500,000
splendidly equipped troops. A little later 25,000
starved, defeated soldiers staggered back.

At the height of the Civil War, Lee invaded the
North. Then came the awful Battle of Gettysburg and the very flower of the Southern Army
retreated southward never to recover.

Here in our gospel Jesus single handed ad-
vances toward Jerusalem. A world redemption
—a world religion hangs in the balance. It is un-
paralelled in the annals of history. And *He*
never retreated. Notice, Jesus goes with a clear
understanding of coming events and with the
vision of a Seer. He goes with readiness to fulfill His Father's will—a soldier of God enduring
the acid test of obedience.

Here then, is a gospel that strengthens our faith
and gives us an example to follow. Remember,
after the cross the crown—after the grave the life
immortal.

REV. MARTIN LUTHER ENDERS, D.D.,
Baltimore, Maryland.

"This is the generation of them that seek him, that seek thy face, O Jacob."—Psalm 24: 6.

THIS is a seeking world. Nature is ever seeking. Flowers and shrubs and trees seek the light. The beasts of the field seek food and shelter. Throughout the long stretch of human history man has been a tireless and continuous seeker. He has sought not only the necessary creature comforts but also a better environment. He has sought knowledge and has contented himself with nothing less than the increasing mastery of the forces of nature.

He has also sought God. With almost a divine restlessness he has been seeking those deeper currents of life which might reveal the Truth more clarly. The search for Truth is even more general today than when David wrote—"This is the generation of them that seek him, that seek thy face, O Jacob." There is but one way by which man's quest of God can be satisfied and that is through Jesus Christ our Lord who said—"I am the way, the truth and the life: no man cometh unto the Father, but by me."

RT. REV. ADNA WRIGHT LEONARD, D.D., LL.D.,
Buffalo, New York.

"Thou wilt keep him in perfect peace, whose mind is stayed on thee: because he trusteth in thee."—Isaiah 26: 3.

AMID confusions of life, the secure anchorage in the Harbor of Trust is the stabilizing persuasion for peace. With this fixidity of faith, whatever the environment, perfect peace is the heavenly portion because the mind is stayed on God. Our Good Shepherd still knows His own; when we hear His Voice, we rest secure in the green pastures by still waters.

The Holy Spirit still comforts: "Peace I leave with you, My peace I give unto you; not as the world giveth, give I unto you. Let not your heart be troubled, neither let it be afraid. . . . These things I have spoken unto you, that in Me ye might have peace. In the world ye shall have tribulation: but be of good cheer; I have overcome the world."

REV. MILTON R. GEARY,
Bangor, Maine.

"For my yoke is easy and my burden is light."—Matthew 11: 30.

LIFE compels us all to bear a yoke. We may choose between the yoke of Christ and the yoke of sin. Whose yoke is heavier, that of the criminal fleeing from the officers of the law, or that of the law-observer, who walks the streets in peace of mind?

The yoke of Christ is easy because He has a way of giving strength to His people. He takes as much of the burden as is above our strength.

The Christian burden is light because it is a burden of love. Love's burden is always light. Here is a mother with a sick babe. She is nurse, mother, housekeeper, and servant all in one. She is able to do the work of two because it is a service of love, and love makes the burden light.

Then life is short. It is soon over. All the heavy burdens we have carried will all seem trifles then.

REV. JOHN NEWTON LACKEY, D.D.,
Hartford, Connecticut.

"This is the way, walk ye in it."—Isaiah 30:21

THIS Message is from the Holy One of Israel to His Chosen People. He calls them Rebellious Children because they were turning from His way of Life and going down to Egypt. They were saying to God's Wise Men "See not"; and to His Prophets, "Prophesy not unto us right things, speak unto us smooth things that will please and deceive us; get you out of the way and turn aside out of God's path, and cause the Holy One of Israel to cease from before us."

God's reply was a Message of mercy and salvation. He said, "I will send my Holy Spirit to whisper in your ear, 'This is the way, walk ye in it.' Listen and return to my way and ye shall be saved, for in quietness and confidence, Faith shall be your strength."

What a picture of world conditions and needs today:—full of unrest and trouble because full of sin and unbelief and defiance of God. God says to us today, "This is the way, walk ye in it."

REV. CLARENCE A. EYLER,
Collingswood, New Jersey.

"In my Father's House are many mansions."—John 14: 2.

GOD HAS given us the Heavenly House. Nothing lovelier has ever come to the mind of man. Only the most beautiful, the most noble things help to make us ready for Heaven.

The picture of Heaven is the most beautiful that has ever been given to the world. Its walls, gates, streets, throne, river are all the most glorious. It is free from sin. In it knowledge is wonderful. It is a home of love. We will know our dear ones who have gone before. We will KNOW Jesus as we have never known Him. Heaven is God's gift to us. If we walk with Jesus we hold fast to the gift.

It is a possession that never fails. It is truest happiness all the way. It has led thousands to smile as death drew near.

If you have a well grounded hope of Heaven you are never really unhappy. If you have the gift never let it go.

REV. LUTHER DE YOE, D.D.,
Germantown, Pennsylvania.

"Cast thy burden upon the Lord, and he shall sustain thee."—Psalm 55: 22.

HAVE you not often been lost in the maze of some staggering anxiety? You have been bewildered. You did not know which way to go, what you could do. You have said, "This burden is more than I can bear." The words of comfort spoken by your friends seemed meaningless. Your very prayers seemed unanswered. Had not God promised to relieve you of your burdens? Why did He not act? Did He say, "I will take away your burden?" This is His promise, "I will carry you and your burden too." "I will sustain thee." Oh, this is the answer! My Lord will give me strength and power to go on. With Paul I now say, "I can do all things through Christ which strengtheneth me."

REV. FREDERICK A. BOWERS, D.D.,
Richmond Hill, New York, N. Y.

"Not as though I had already attained, either were already perfect: but I follow after, if that I may apprehend that for which also I am apprehended of Christ Jesus."—Philippians 3:12.

THE LURE of the unattained is strong and irresistible. It has conquered mountains, penetrated jungles, discovered new continents. It impelled St. Paul to blaze a trail of light that has shined with beneficent splendor across the years. Its marching music thrills to the words.

Its supreme requisite is a strong, resolute faith. No faint hearts need apply. He who disbelieves is lost. But he who faces life with this quiet resolve, "Though he slay me, yet will I trust in him," is on the upward ascent, gaining new glimpses and experiencing new glories.

The rejuvenating power of Christ's redeeming love; the fadeless beauty of Christian character; the immeasurable influence of a life geared to the world's need—all are realized through faith. "Friend, come up higher," is the gracious plea of Christ to every aspiring life. With the heights before you, with life's best ahead of you, press on.

REV. SAMUEL R. CURRY,
Ashland, Kentucky.

"He showed them his hands and his feet."—Luke 24: 40.

BEAUTIFUL carpenter hands that had used spokeshave, drawing-knife, adze and saw; that had made yokes easy for shoulders of man and beast. Hands that broke bread for the hungry; had brought strength to withered hands; that tenderly touched the heads of little children. Feet that walked the country road, village and city streets, and climbed the mountain to the place of prayer. Many could testify to the kindness of those hands and the beauty of the feet of him who brought good news of God.

But cruel men caused nails to be driven through those hands and feet; and Jesus had suffered the excruciating pains of crucifixion.

To the disciples, later, he showed his (own) hands and his (own) feet. We think that a glad joy and a divine pride were on his face. In that look there is still a challenge—a challenge with a commensurate inspiration. His disciples today might well envy those scars!

REV. WILLIAM HINTS, B D., D.D.,
Salt Lake City, Utah.

"God hath said, I will dwell in them, and walk in them; and I will be their God, and they shall be my people."— 2 Corinthians 6: 16.

THERE are not many things the world needs more than it needs people who walk and talk with God.

A Christian ought to live such a helpful, kind life, that as folks see him walking along the way they will instinctively feel "there goes God—walking and living in that man."

A heathen girl was so deeply impressed with the sweet, loving character of a missionary that she yearned for—"the beautiful life." She soon found that it was the Christ-life that she wanted.

Let us walk and talk with God, then when Christ comes He can say, "Well done, good and faithful servant." Matt. 25: 21.

REV. M. G. DICKINSON, PH.B.,
Brookville, Pennsylvania.

"But he that prophesieth speaketh unto men to edification, and exhortation, and comfort."—1 Corinthians 14: 3.

PROPHECY, in the sense of this text, is just
God's message to men and especially to Christian men. It is said to be for their edification,
exhortation and comfort, or in the quaint language of Canon Shore, for building up, stirring
up, and cheering up. God's message is for "building up." The Christian life is like a building;
you neglect a building; it may be the finest and
fairest of mansions, but if you neglect it for a
time, it will soon run down and become dilapi-
dated. We must keep building it up, cleaning it,
beautifying it, else it will in course of time fall
into utter ruin. We must take the same care of
our souls or they, too, fall into ruin. God's message is needed to build us up in our faith. That
is why it is so important to attend regularly and
faithfully to the preaching of God's word.

REV. CHARLES H. STEWART, D.D.,
Buffalo, New York.

"Again I say unto you, That if two of you shall agree on earth as touching anything that they shall ask, it shall be done for them of my Father which is in Heaven. For where two or three are gathered together in my name, there am I in the midst of them."—Matthew 18: 19, 20.

MORE than forty years ago, while a student at Gettysburg College, the President, Dr. McKnight, brought this message to my attention. The story he told of its fulfillment for himself and his wife in a great emergency, made a deep impression. Throughout all my ministry this Scripture passage has been put to practical use. We have had marvelous results therefrom in our own home life. We have used it constantly in the planting and developing of more than fifty churches. I have given it to thousands of people in my daily contacts with them, applying it to all of life's problems.

Dear friend, challenge its fulfillment. The only condition is: "If two of you shall agree," *for the glory of God.*

REV. S. D. DAUGHERTY, D.D.,
Philadelphia, Pennsylvania.

"When I became a man, I put away childish things."
—1 Corinthians 13: 11.

LET us resolve to grow up into a state of SPIRITUAL MATURITY.

How many childish things we have held onto since we became "new creatures in Christ Jesus"! How loath we are to give up the baubles which dazzled us before Jesus came into our hearts! What fairy tales of error we still delight to hear! How easily Satan deceives us by the fine voices and fine phrases of Falsehood!

Let us put away childish things and become full grown Christians. But you will say, How shall I grow up? By assiduous study of the Word of God, wrestling mightily in prayer, and "not forsaking the assembling of ourselves together."

Here are some of the pleasures of Spiritual Maturity: Consciousness of the completeness of our Salvation. Consciousness of our intimate association with Christ here in this life, and consciousness of the unutterable joys awaiting us in Glory.

REV. WALTER F. MCMILLIN, D.D.,
Minneapolis, Minnesota.

"But they that wait upon the Lord shall renew their strength; they shall mount up with wings as eagles; they shall run, and not be weary; and they shall walk, and not faint."—Isaiah 40: 31.

IN A world where God is at work, waiting is more important than doing. Our spiritual life demands worship as well as work. Out from aloneness with God, Jesus came to work for man. At the end of the weary day's work of helping, healing and redeeming He was wont to return to the quiet place of prayer, communion and renewal that He might be prepared for the morrow's task. What an example for us! The great souls that have pierced the mystery and perfected the mastery of life have been much alone with God. Prayer is the promise of progress. If we are to be kept from work in the world, we must have what Isaiah had—vision, poise and patience, and these come to the souls of men through meditation and prayer.

RT. REV. WALLACE E. BROWN,
Helena, Montana.

"The Father sent the Son to be the Savior of the World."
—1 John 4: 14.

THAT text simply tells everything. It sounds
the note that gives the Bible its chief value,
the church its abiding mission, and guarantees
glory to every believer.

The very fact of it! How wonderful! Salvation. My salvation. Not just a few bad habits
to put away, but made a new creature. That's
why He is a Savior, and what He came here and
is enthroned yonder for. And our New Testament's defined task is to tell it to the world. The
Saviorhood of Jesus. Let us make that our chief
concern. All else that may fill and thrill, is as
nothing in comparison.

"This great and glorious Gospel
We're summoned to proclaim,
Brings full and free salvation,
Through faith in Jesus' name."

REV. JOSEPH LYONS EWING, D.D.,
Rahway, New Jersey.

"Be of good cheer; I have overcome the world."——John 16: 33.

HOW inappropriate and untrue these words seemed when they were uttered. The world was apparently about to defeat our Master. The plans for His arrest and death on the following day were in process of execution. The Savior was not ignorant of these plans. To the betrayer He had said: "What thou doest, do quickly." He told His disciples plainly that His death was approaching. Facing apparent defeat, Christ said, "Be of good cheer; I have overcome the world."

Sometimes we hear disciples wondering whether God's Redemptive Plan will be frustrated. Frequently we hear them praying that victory for Christ may come. All such disciples should heed our Lord's words, "I have overcome the world." Victory is not in doubt. Victory is not in the future. Victory was won centuries ago. The world and sin at their worst were mastered by Christ on and immediately after Calvary.

RT. REV. ERNEST G. RICHARDSON,
Philadelphia, Pennsylvania.

"The dayspring from on high hath visited us, to give light to them that sit in darkness."—Luke 1: 78–79.

NIGHT had settled about our race, but the coming of Christ meant the dawning of a new day. Clement of Alexandria had this in mind when he wrote, "He hath turned all our sunsets into sunrise." Consider some of the ways in which He has turned sunset into sunrise. He turned the sunset of human groping after God into the sunrise of Divine Certainty. He turned the sunset of dreary pessimism into the sunrise of glad hope. Thus we believe that, "Somewhere night drifts to a morning beautiful with light." He turned the sunset of earthly sorrow into the sunrise of heavenly comfort. He turned the sunset of sin's destruction into the sunrise of complete redemption. He turned the sunset of death's shadows into the sunrise of immortal day.

REV. CHARLES P. MACGREGOR,
Concord, New Hampshire.

"Take away this cup from me: nevertheless not what I will, but what thou wilt."—Mark 14:36.

IT IS well known that we enter the crises and the sacred experiences of our lives alone. There are seasons we seem to be on a lonely raft at sea, far removed from society. We wave at distant ships for help, and so often they fail to see our signals.

Some of life's solitudes are tragic. In solitude we sin, and in solitude we repent. There is the solitude of old age, and the solitude of great seekers after truth. Our prophets and seers who lead us into the revealed purposes of God, know something of solitude. Amid the suffering of solitude Christ made the final surrender.

Many of life's solitudes are triumphant. They lead us into a richer and deeper understanding of God's will for us, and bring us ultimately into a more hallowed communion, and nobler avenues of service. The garden faithfulness will lead to the garden fellowships.

REV. H. H. BINGHAM, B.A., D.D.,
Toronto, Ontario, Canada.

"Speak unto the children of Israel, that they go forward."
—Exodus 14: 15.

THE Israelites, erstwhile slaves of Pharaoh, in their flight, find themselves in a sorry case. Before them lies the Red Sea. It effectually bars the way to the Promised Land of peace and safety. Behind them flash in the sunlight the warlike accoutrements of Pharaoh's advancing host and the sight strikes terror into their hearts.

O, cruel dilemma! The Egyptians or the Red Sea! Certain woe or God must do the impossible! They cry to Moses in their extremity and he answers them out of the mouth of God: "Speak unto the children of Israel, that they go forward."

In the face of difficulty, we must go forward. Problems are not solved by repining. Indeed, they grow larger and blacker as we dwell upon them. Faith justifies itself to the faithful. Go forward! God will surely go with you to open and smooth the way, for nothing is impossible with Him.

REV. REESE F. THORNTON, S.T.B.,
Lafayette, Indiana.

"The Lord is my strength and song."—Psalm 118: 14.

EVEN before God gave us the supreme source of joy in Jesus Christ the noblest souls of Israel knew that to possess God was to carry a song in one's heart.

All the everyday joys of life, the beauty of God's world, the satisfaction in work well done, the love of friends and home, are enriched by the presence of God.

But it is when times are hard and work is drudgery and the world is dark that we know most truly that God is our song. We turn to Christ and in Him know that God's love surrounds us, tender and strong and sustaining. The divine Song bursts out through sorrow and trouble and hardship. Happy is the man who carries that song in his heart.

RT. REV. EDWARD L. PARSONS, D.D.,
San Francisco, California.

"I am crucified with Christ: nevertheless I live; yet not I, but Christ liveth in me: and the life which I now live in the flesh, I live by the faith of the Son of God, who loved me, and gave himself for me."—Galatians 2: 20.

BLESSED, holy mystery! Divinity intruded into humanity. The old Adam having been crucified is dead to sin. The new man lives and reigns within. The new creature though still in the flesh, lives the new life, the same divine life that was so real to the Son of Man; and appropriates by faith the merits and character of Him who loved him and gave Himself for him.

Scripture texts are like doors to a house. This precious scripture is a golden gate open wide. The believer who enters in, finds himself in the inner sanctuary of God's love.

Step in, O trustful child of God, and receive comfort, cheer, courage, strength for service, and grace for grace.

REV. M. P. HOCKER, D.D.,
Ambler, Pennsylvania.

"I am the way, and the truth, and the life."—John 14: 6.

THE man who builds his hopes on the sandy incidentals of Christianity, ignoring the Rock of Ages, is on dangerous ground. The changes of time and fortune may sever ecclesiastical connections and incite to the breaking of moral resolutions and the ignoring of ethical ideals, but they make sweeter and stronger the life-ties between Jesus and His own.

I met an aged invalid in the wilds of the mountains. When I was introduced to him as a minister, for a moment it seemed as if the enthusiasm of youth had come back to his failing body as he clasped my hand and said—"It has been thirty years since I heard a sermon or was inside of a church, but while my helpless life here has compelled me to break with all my old associations, I still feel the grip of my Savior's hand. Jesus and I are better friends than ever. They say that I could not live a month if they took me away from this mountain air, but I would not want to live a day if I were separated from Him."

REV. FORREST F. DAGER, D.D.,
Philadelphia, Pennsylvania.

"David encouraged himself in the Lord his God."—1 Samuel 30: 6.

THE world is full of discouraged people. You find them everywhere. It is no reproach to one's character to be discouraged, but it is a reflection on one's good judgment not to seek sources of encouragement.

Everybody who is normal has been bewildered by circumstances and asked in soliloquy, "Oh, what shall I do?"

David's experience gives us the best lead on the way out of such a quandary. "He encouraged himself in the Lord his God."

The Lord our God can help us too. He can transform our fears into courage, our doubts into trust, and our defeats into victories.

His promise never fails, "Call upon me in the day of trouble, and I will deliver thee."

REV. ROY C. HELFENSTEIN, M.A., B.D., D.D., *Dover, Delaware.*

"And it shall come to pass, that before they call, I will answer; and while they are yet speaking, I will hear."— Isaiah 65:24.

A PAINTER, who, reduced to very straitened circumstances and believing in seeking help from God "in the day of trouble," carried his distressing situation to God in prayer, asking God to send, if possible and in harmony with His will, a purchaser for his painting, "The Angel Uriel."

While he was yet on his knees a man came and inquired the price and paid the artist even more than he expected for the somewhat celebrated painting, for it had received one of the prizes at the Royal Academy.

The artist whose fame soon after spread around the world, testified in later years that the encouragement which came to him in the sale of this picture had more than anything else to do with starting him on the way to his brilliant career.

Is it too much to believe that God knew the needy artist was going to pray and had his benefactor on the way before the painter was on his knees? Has he not said, "Before they call, I will answer?"

REV. WILLIAM EDWARD BIEDERWOLF,
Palm Beach, Florida.

"It shall be given you in that same hour"—Matthew 10: 19.

THE Master knew how natural this fear is. He knew that His disciples would be obliged to face experiences, not unlike His own. He knew that they might be consumed with anxious worry as to how they would meet the issue. "When they deliver you up" He said, "take no thought how or what ye shall speak: for it shall be given you in that same hour what ye shall speak."

To those who are afraid of being afraid, the promise will come true.

There is a strength as well as a peace which passes understanding. It comes in the hour of need to those who have tasted that the Lord is gracious. There are revelations of God which can be known only when God is needed most. There are capacities for receiving God which are undiscovered until one is compelled to call out of the deep. This is the antidote against the fear of being afraid.

REV. ROMILLY F. HUMPHRIES, D.D.,
Archdeacon of Baltimore, Maryland.

"If ye abide in me, and my words abide in you, ye shall ask what ye will, and it shall be done unto you."—John 15: 7.

YEARS ago an old Indian frequently visited one of our military camps and begged for money. He wore an old locket and the men became curious to know what it contained. On opening it they found there a parchment on which was written a pension and signed by George Washington. The old Indian did not know he had it. Thus many have a signed pension from God and do not realize it.

We are told the juice of the fruit and the sap of the vine are the same. The Spirit of the Christ and of the Christian are the same. You can tell where the vine stops and the branch begins but there is a union and a similarity. The closer we abide in Him the greater this will be. This is accomplished by having His word abide in us. May we know His language and speak in His accent that when we call upon Him He will know that we are His and our prayers will be answered. Then plenty is guaranteed us.

REV. JOHN BORLAND CAVITT, PH.D.,
Albuquerque, New Mexico.

"And when they had lifted up their eyes, they saw no man, save Jesus only."—Matthew 17: 8.

THE Transfiguration of Jesus came not for Him alone but rather for His Chosen Disciples who needed strength and faith in their future work of Kingdom Building. We, too, know some of the blessings that come from our mountain top experiences and like Peter, we would love to have tarried there forever with Jesus. But the world awaits our work and our witness bearing.

When people are forgetting God and neglecting His church it is our task to bring the nations of the earth to the Christ, that they may know no one save Jesus only. For "Jesus only" remains the greatest historical person of all ages; the greatest teacher among men and the greatest religious founder of all time. He is "yesterday, today, and forever the same."

The weary and turbulent world will never find rest and peace until they turn to Jesus only and hear Him speak, "PEACE BE STILL."

REV. PARK W. HUNTINGTON, A.M., B.D., *Wilmington, Delaware.*

"I will both lay me down in peace, and sleep: for thou, Lord, only makest me dwell in safety."—Psalms 4 : 8.

I HEARD him singing early in the morning. It was hardly light! I could not understand that song; it was fairly a lilt of joy. It had been a portentous night for me, full of dreams that did disturb me. Old things that I had hoped to forget and new things that I had prayed would never come, trouped through my dreams all grinning like little bare-faced imps. Certainly I was in no humor to sing. What could possess that fellow out yonder to be telling the whole township how joyous he was? He was perched on the old rail fence by the spring run. He was drenched. It had rained in the night and evidently he had been poorly housed. I pitied him. What comfort could he have had through that night bathed in storm? He never thought of comfort. His song was not bought by any such duplicity. It was in his heart. He could do no other. Then I shook myself. The shame that a lark had finer poise than a man!

REV. G. A. LEICHLITER, M.A., B.D.,
Toronto, Ontario, Canada.

"Simon, behold, Satan hath desired to have you, that he may sift you as wheat, but I have prayed for thee, that thy *faith fail not.*"—Luke 22: 31, 32.

CHRIST did not pray that Peter might have more wisdom, courage, piety, veracity, all of which he needed. He prayed that his *"Faith Fail Not."*

In the hour of Peter's disillusionment and sore discouragement, the supreme test would be upon his faith in himself, in the church, in Christ. There was his great peril. Hence Christ's prayer. In the crucial experiences of life the great steadying, saving thing is faith. "Faith is the victory that overcometh." The peril of Christian men in this intimidating age is a loss of faith. Let nothing rob you of your faith in yourself, in your church, in your Christ. Believe—it is God's great imperative, it is man's great salvation.

REV. WILLIAM R. KING, D.D.,
New York, New York.

"There remaineth therefore a rest to the people of God."
—Hebrews 4: 9.

WHEN God uses the word "rest" He means freedom from anything that wearies or troubles,—peace of mind. To be free from labor does not insure rest. A man in jail has no labor, but he also has no rest. "The way of the transgressor is hard." It is not work that kills, but worry. When a man is in tune with the Infinite, his mind is at peace and his heart is free from grief because God cares and shares. That is what Jesus meant when He said, "Come unto Me all ye that labor . . . and ye shall have *rest unto your souls.*"

Soul-rest, that's what humanity needs. Are you bowed down beneath the weight of life? Come to Jesus. Under His yoke life can reach its highest and achieve its best.

REV. DALLAS C. BAER, A.M., B.D.,
Selinsgrove, Pennsylvania.

"But he knoweth the way that I take: when he hath tried me, I shall come forth as gold."—Job 23: 10.

JOB could not understand his trials but he could "Trust." The Lord said, "There is none like him in the earth, a perfect and an upright man, one that feareth God and escheweth evil." Satan disputed God's confidence in Job but the Lord knew the heart of His servant and used him to defeat the purpose of the devil. Job knew how to approach a crisis—"When the crisis comes, *He* will tell *me* how to rest; *He* will tell *me* what to do; *He* will tell *me* what to say."

Our extremity is God's opportunity. Perhaps our Lord is challenging the Devil about us. Is our faith like the old patriarch's? Can we say "I know that my Redeemer liveth"?

"Testimony" is Christianity in action.

SAMUEL R. BOGGS,
Philadelphia, Pennsylvania.

"Ye must be born again."—John 3:7.

EVERY known form of life is born anew with transformation from above. The germinating seed, reaching down its fingers of life, translates elements of soil and rock into the vegetable kingdom. The vital animal principle of the cow changes vegetable food into animal nature. The intelligence of the creator touches matter, and thinking man is here.

The chemist may work upon mineral matter for ages: without a previously created germ he cannot develop life. A Burbank may change many forms of plant life. No human arrangement can develop a vegetable into the animal kingdom. Trainers of animals develop wondrous traits. They cannot produce rationality where it does not inhere. The leaven of the Holy Spirit alone gives life to a soul born from above.

REV. G. R. HEIM,
Loysville, Pennsylvania.

"For the eyes of the Lord run to and fro throughout the whole earth, to shew himself strong in the behalf of them whose heart is perfect toward him."—2 Chronicles 16: 9.

THIS message came to me during many nights when I could not sleep, that I really did not care so much about sleep. Those restless nights became sessions of great joy. To know that my loving heavenly Father was constantly watching over me, constantly with me, and constantly taking every opportunity to strengthen and bless my spirit and body, was an enriching joy and comfort to me, and had greatly to do with my recovery from illness. Ever since that time I have been joyous in this consciousness of the knowledge and personal interest and ready help of my loving heavenly Father. Indeed, I have ever since been rather glad that that illness came to me, because of this blessed discovery and this happy fellowship with God.

The word "perfect," used here, does not mean "sinlessness," but "sincerity." To the man who is sincere in his relation to God, willing to be a true friend, God's eyes are always on him, in sweetest love, ever watching for every opportunity to come into his life to befriend, to encourage, to help in all the fullness of His grace.

REV. S. WILLIS McKELVEY, D.D.. *Kansas City, Missouri.*

"But by the grace of God I am what I am; and his grace which was bestowed upon me was not in vain."—I Corinthians 15: 10.

PERSONALITY is not the product of one little lifetime. God has been at work for ages upon the personality of each of us through his great laws of heredity. The result is that in all this world there are no two persons exactly alike—never have been and never will be.

What does this mean? You are God's opportunity in your day. He has waited ages for a person just like you. If you are yielded to him and his will is being performed through you, then God is having his opportunity. If you refuse him, then God loses his opportunity which he sought through you and he will never have another for there will never be another person on earth just like you.

REV. CHARLES F. MAYHEW,
Arlington, New Jersey.

"O the depth of the riches both of the wisdom and knowledge of God: how unsearchable are his judgments, and his ways past finding out!"—Romans 11: 33.

A N OWL who had so successfully dominated the mice in his barn, that he felt himself to be a ruling spirit in the universe, by some mischance was out in the open air at noon on a summer day. Dazzled and pained by the light of the Sun, he fluttered home as best he could and thus complained to his mate: "The Sun is nature's great mistake; it dries up the delightful little pools; it makes the weeds grow, fills the air with fog, and gives poor farmers the sunstroke. What a pity it can't be done away with! Then we should always have soothing night, so grateful to our eyes." So the beneficent Sun, that gives vitality to our planet, ripens our crops, fills our morning and evening skies with glory and holds the Earth in its orbit is regarded by the Owl. So is Theism derided by the Skeptic.

REV. CARL ECKHARDT GRAMMER, S.T.D.,
Philadelphia, Pennsylvania.

"Men ought always to pray."—Luke 18: 1.

OUR age demands we "Be brief, bright and breezy." Man's popular excuse is "I'm so busy." The result is we forget our true sources of strength. An old saint once said, "If a man is so busy that he has no time for prayer, he is busier than God Almighty ever intended." Surely, we need the refreshment that God alone can give.

Returning from Chicago, I noticed between the tracks, long, narrow trenches of water. I asked the man in the chair alongside of me as to their purpose. He answered, "This flier cannot take time to stop for water. She must scoop it up as she rushes along."

So we, hurrying along life's way, can scoop up strength by looking to God in prayer.

REV. IVAN H. HAGEDORN,
Collingswood, New Jersey.

"That which we have, seen and heard declare we unto you also, that ye may have fellowship with us: yea, and our fellowship is with the Father, and with his son Jesus Christ."—1 John 1: 3. Revised Version.

ST. JOHN writes we heard the voice of the eternal Son of God. We heard Him speak words of comfort, truth, love, and life.

We heard the Sermon on the Mount and those precious addresses delivered by Him, during the last week of His life. We saw Him work Miracles, even raise the dead to life. We saw Him living again after His death.

That which the disciples had heard and had seen they declared unto us, that we should have fellowship with them, the Father and His Son Jesus Christ, and that we should realize the fullness of joy. This joy is reciprocal between the disciples and ourselves.

Surely our faith is quickened when we realize the disciples sought neither wealth nor power and suffered persecution, even death, to tell us about Jesus.

REV. CHARLES L. QUINN,
Oldwick, New Jersey.

"The Lord is able to give thee much more than this."— 2 Chronicles 25 : 9.

WHEN Lot was given his choice he took the well watered plains, but God chose for Abraham the hills where he found a place to build an altar.

Daniel purposed in his heart not to defile himself with the king's meat and the Lord gave him much more than the richest banquet table could provide. The heroes of faith testify that God is faithful. They held back their hand from selfish indulgence and God gave them His royal bounty.

We sometimes feel shut out of pleasures because they do not seem appropriate to our Christian profession. We almost believe that we are martyrs and we seek for some justification whereby we might engage in these things and still hold the approval of our conscience.

But the Lord has an overflowing cup to satisfy our deepest desires. The good works that He has prepared for us to walk in bring joy of heart and peace of soul.

REV. H. F. MARTIN, PH.D., D.D.,
Fremont, Nebraska.

"This is life eternal, that they might know Thee the only true God."—John 17: 3.

I KNOW God by the exercise of my reason, as I know of the ether, atoms, electrons, and other invisibles.

I know God by faith, as I know a noted man whom I have never seen; through the testimony of those who do know him, through his words and his works.

I know God through fellowship; the fellowship of speech, through reading His Word, and talking with Him in prayer; the fellowship of work, because I am working together with Him to accomplish certain ends; the fellowship of Love, for Love opens channels of communion, otherwise closed.

This knowledge satisfies my reason, my faith, my emotions. It surpasses all external testimony. With the Psalmist I cry, "O taste and see that the Lord is good!"

REV. GEORGE C. ALBORN,
Bricelyn, Minnesota.

"Let not your heart be troubled."—John 14: 1.

IT IS not God's thought to trouble His children. We are not to call trouble what we experience through God's dealings with us. Sometimes He chastens us; sometimes He enlivens our spirits with signal blessings.

If we know ourselves to be God's children, we can see God in the shadows which we call our troubles.

It is the fall of the year. The waters lie a placid pool. On them we see the deep shadows of the hillsides. We look away from the shadows and see the beauty of riotous colors glorifying them. That which we see shadowed in the waters are objects of marvelous beauty. Let us look away from the shadows of life and see God in His effulgent and beneficent splendor.

REV. THOMAS REISCH, D.D.,
Harrisburg, Pennsylvania.

"I waited patiently for the Lord . . . and He heard my cry. He set my feet upon a rock . . . and put a new song in my mouth."—Psalm 40: 1 3.

WE ARE living in an age of impatience, insisting upon high speed transportation, demanding quick service in business. We expect short sermons and look for immediate answers to our prayers. Patience is a virtue. The Bible tells us that we should be patient even in tribulations, that all who wait upon the Lord will be strengthened.

Patience is a form of discipline. Jesus Christ is the ideal example of this. Impatience never lingered in His heart. Patient waiting upon God was a common practice of our Lord. It brought forth from His lips the amazing statement, "Father forgive them, they know not what they do." It enabled Him to conquer death, even the death of the cross, to redeem man from sin to Life Eternal.

Patience assures us that God will hear our cry, that we will be lifted up and our feet planted firmly upon a rock, that a new song will be put in our mouth. Blessed is the man who maketh the Lord his trust, who waits patiently upon the Lord.

REV. JACOB E. RUDISILL,
Philadelphia, Pennsylvania

"A good man shall be satisfied from himself."—Proverbs 14: 14.

THE soul's great quest is for satisfaction. It ranges the heavens and the earth in search of that which will secure rest.

Considering only the earnest soul that is not content with things only earthly, there is demanded: Truth, that is comprehensive and therefore capable of regulating thought and life, and that is inexhaustible and therefore secures progress; Perfect Love, untainted by selfishness; and a Conscience that is purified and enlightened.

Sometimes the mistake is made of thinking that these satisfying elements may be generated within man. The teaching of the Holy Scriptures is that the power for the acquisition of all that finally satisfies comes from God.

To be satisfied one must "drink from his own cistern," not another's. The cistern is filled by the rains of Heaven. But the cistern is one's own. It is my Faith, my Devotion, my Trust which will give the deep satisfaction that stabilizes and comforts my soul.

REV. WALTER W. EDGE, D.D.,
Lancaster, Pennsylvania.

"Thou wilt keep him in perfect peace, whose mind is stayed on thee: because he trusteth in thee."—Isaiah 26: 3.

LISTEN to Jesus the eternal Son of God: "In the world ye shall have tribulation, but in Me ye shall have peace." In Him alone we have PEACE.

When petty annoyances try to inject themselves into your mind and disorganize your program, let the peace of Christ acting as your traffic officer compel them to get out of the way for more important work. He will surely protect us and guide us, and help us in every time of need. Our only concern should be . . . is He FIRST in our lives?

In every place we who trust God and His Christ . . . we are not ALONE. God is here and the result of His PRESENCE is PERFECT PEACE.

REV. WALTER L. HUNT,
Camden, New Jersey.

"He leadeth me."—Psalms 23:2.

HAVE you ever realized that iron and steel are essentially the same—the only difference being the experience of fire? Yet, iron as such is almost useless. The skyscrapers, bridges, steamers and a thousand more of man's modern achievements have been made possible because iron has been changed into steel.

Man is but the iron of humanity. It is not until he has been changed by the experience of God that he becomes the steel of Christianity.

Sometimes the road by which He leads us is hard and rough. Sometimes we have doubts as to where He is leading us and we want to quit and go back. His leading may include poverty, sickness, death and loss of friends. But only by following His leading continuously do we become the steel of which it is possible for Him to create the finer structures of Christianity.

REV. ALFORD R. NAUS,
Camden, New Jersey.

"I will make all my mountains a way."—Isaiah 49: 11.

A RELIGION that enables us to change a mountain into a highway is the only religion for us. Israel had been overcome by the foe and her people carried away. But God had not forsaken them. Their years of servitude was his way of training them for their high mission among the nations. Through the mountain of bondage they had discovered a more spiritual view of God.

We admire the courage of a Tyndall who made the Matterhorn a pass from Italy to Switzerland. But we worship in the name of One who made Mount Calvary a new and living way into the presence of God. In His faith we can transform the greatest obstacles into means for the attainment of true life and character.

REV. MURDOCH MACKINNON, M.A., D.D.,
Toronto, Ontario. Canada

"But we all, with open face beholding as in a glass the glory of the Lord, are changed into the same image from glory to glory, even as by the Spirit of the Lord."—2 Corinthians 3: 18.

CHRIST is God's mirror. When He is in our hearts we see ourselves as we ought to be. But we must remove the veil of sin and fill our minds with what is true and honorable, pure and lovely. We must go about doing good, forgetting what is behind and running the upward race. Then God's ultra-violet rays of faith, hope and love will shine through us and transfigure us, and all our path will blossom with the beautiful flowers and fruits of the Spirit. We shall be a daily living sacrifice to change things as they are into things as they ought to be, and we shall have no fear, for our life is hid with Christ in God, and there the tooth of time cannot touch us.

REV. RAYMOND T. STAMM, PH.D.,
Gettysburg, Pennsylvania.

"How precious also are Thy thoughts unto me, O God! how great is the sum of them."—Psalm 139: 17.

GOD'S thoughts! Like flashing gems are they, and great is the sum of them. The thoughts of the Divine Intelligence guide the universe. He thinks in the large, yet concretely too. "He calleth His own . . . by name."

True and beautiful are God's thoughts, nor can man fathom their depth; more brilliant than the diamond's fire, richer than the ruby's glow. Yet His are compassionate thoughts, noting the sorrow, pain, folly, sin that mar the life of His child.

God's supreme thought is a saving one—Calvary. Deep it is, full of tears, suffering unto death, redemptive by His own passion, a thought of love so excelling that He Himself can think no greater. The cross of Christ is God's most precious thought for men.

REV. JOHN EDWARD BUSHNELL, D.D.,
Minneapolis, Minnesota.

"Prove me now herewith, saith the Lord of hosts, if I will not open you the windows of heaven, and pour you out a blessing, that there shall not be room enough to receive it."—Malachi 3: 10.

WE ARE living in an age of Guaranteed Merchandise. When we go to the Jeweler, the Automobile Salesman or even to our Clothier we want to know something of the goods which we buy. We want to get full value for our money. Men will trust a company which has proven the value of its products, but man is not willing to trust a God Who for thousands of years has been supplying the needs of the entire world. Take God at His Word. Prove Him, and the blessings from Heaven will not only fall upon you but upon your family, your friends and all with whom you associate.

REV. DON L. MARSH,
Brooklyn, New York.

"Let not your heart be troubled: ye believe in God, believe also in me."—John 14: 1.

MERE belief in the existence of God is not enough. We must believe in Jesus Christ, the eternal Son of God, whom God, the Father, has sacrificed for our redemption in order that we may be saved.

Having believed in Christ and secured instantaneous and eternal salvation, we are assured of protection in this life and provision of the next life. In that heavenly locality we are to be in constant companionship, fellowship and conversational relationship to Jesus Christ, who died that we might be saved.

He said these things will be accomplished in order that we might be with Him. He desires to have His church, His saints, His redeemed subjects with Him in the glory world. We shall be with Him and dwell with Him forever.

Glorious is the news, the comfort, and the happiness derived from these facts.

REV. MARK A. MATTHEWS, D.D., LL.D.,
Seattle, Washington.

"The Kingdoms of this world are become the kingdoms of our Lord, and of his Christ."—Revelation 11: 15.

IT IS a rash thing to claim a victory while the battle is still in progress. Yet it is no unreal phantasy, but a true vision that is here revealed. The triumph has been won. The living Christ, risen, ascended, knows no defeat. Nor do we, if we fight in His strength, and under His leadership.

What a glorious promise, and it is ours. And what a glorious privilege to share with our Lord the joy of His conquest. And what a blessed assurance of the ultimate, nay, of the present, sovereignty of righteousness. Illness, temptation, sorrows, within, evil and fear, without, are all subject to His power. "He shall reign for ever and ever." And in all things, we too are "more than conquerors," through Him who saves us.

REV. T. STANNAGE BOYLE, D.D., D.C.L.,
Cobourg, Ontario, Canada.

"God is love . . ."—1 John 4: 16.

ONE of the elemental demands of our natures for fullness of life is friendship, comradeship, love.

Happily most of us have an abundance of it. Home relationships, particularly, provide it in profusion and he who knows it there, needs not St. Paul to tell him that it is "the greatest thing in the world."

But the Apostle was not altogether correct in saying that "love never faileth." The sad truth is that comrades forsake comrades, friendships turn to hatreds, great loves cease to be.

If only there might be, then, some love which actually endureth beyond all possibility of decay, one like that of which George Matheson sings:

"O love that wilt not let me go!"

There is such a love! God is love.

REV. RALPH D. HEIM, PH.D.,
Greenville, Pennsylvania.

"Who shall separate us from the love of Christ? shall tribulation, or distress, or persecution, or famine, or nakedness, or peril, or sword?—Romans 8: 35.

EVERY man must make some kind of an assumption by which he will live his life. Shall that assumption be that at heart the universe is good, or shall we assume that it is evil? Is life in the grip of love or does some malevolent power hold it in bondage? Paul's choice was final and absolute. He assumed that God is love and that there are no creatures or powers in the universe that could separate him from that love.

If the sense of security is essential to the peace and comfort of nations, it is equally imperative in the life of the individual. If God is for us, who can be against us? If His love is secure, what further protection can one need or want?

REV. CHARLES E. CREITZ, D.D.,
Reading, Pennsylvania.

"But my God shall supply all your need, according to his riches in glory by Christ Jesus."—Philippians 4: 19.

THE GRACE of God is marked by the abundance which characterizes all His works. What an abundance of light and warmth in the sun that has shone for so many thousands of years And yet there is no appearance of exhaustion or decay! What an abundance of stars spread over the sky; of leaves that cover the forest; of raindrops; of dews that sparkle on the grass; of snowflakes that cover the hills; of the flowers that adorn the meadow; of all living creatures walking on the ground, playing in the waters, burrowing in the earth, dancing in the sunlight, flying in the air, finding a home in every element.

This lavish profusion of life, and forms, and beauty, in nature is an emblem and proof of the abundance of the grace of God.

In Christ all fullness dwells. We are complete in Him. And in His Spirit there is sufficient power to cleanse the foulest, and break the hardest heart.

REV. W. F. CALDWELL,
Maynard, Iowa.

"In nothing be anxious; but in everything by prayer and supplication with thanksgiving let your requests be made known unto God."—Philippians 4: 6. Revised Version.

IN NOTHING . . . in everything." Let *nothing* give you anxious care; take *everything* to God. He will supply every need according to His riches in glory in Christ Jesus. If anybody had justification for worry, Paul had. In 2 Corinthians, Chapters 11 and 12, he gives us glimpses of his trials, perils, and sufferings. When he exhorted the Philippians to be anxious in nothing, he was a prisoner in Rome. Chained to a soldier he could say, "I have learned, in whatsoever state I am, therein to be content." Would we learn the secret of untroubled hearts? Here it is in the verse we study today. Do not fret, do not worry, do not be anxious; carry everything to God in prayer, cast all your anxieties upon Him, for He careth for you. Commit thy way unto the Lord; trust also in Him and He will bring it to pass.

REV. E. C. ROUTH, D.D.,
Oklahoma City, Oklahoma.

"I also could speak as ye do: if your soul were in my soul's stead, I could heap up words against you, and shake mine head at you."—Job 16: 4.

IF WE want to be helpful in life one of the most essential things is to be able to put ourselves in the other man's place and get his viewpoint. Job's comforters were of little use because they were unable to understand Job and his sorrow. When we put ourselves in the other man's place and understand his problems we will not join words against him, we will help.

Jesus Christ is the One who has done this supremely. His soul has been in our soul's stead. In order to get our viewpoint He left heaven. He was tempted in all points like we are. He suffered and toiled as a man. He knows our problems. He died in our stead. He is able to help. He is willing to help. Let us give Him our confidence and He will help.

REV. F. PAUL McCONKEY, D.D.,
Detroit, Michigan.

"Only do lead a life that is worthy of the gospel of Christ. Whether I come and see you or only hear of you in absence, let me know that you are standing firm in a common spirit, fighting side by side like one man for the faith of the gospel."—Philippians 1:27. Moffatt.

IN THESE days it is no easy matter to lead a life "worthy of the gospel of Christ." And yet that is exactly what is needed. We call this a Christian land and yet in industry, politics, education, and religion we fall far short of the principles of Jesus. We call ourselves "Christians" and there are lynchings and social prejudice and un-neighborliness.

So, as I think of you who are reading, may we not have the joy of knowing of each other that we are doing each our level best to stand firm in a common spirit? May we not pledge each other, in the spirit of Jesus, to live each day to the full; being our own selves at our very best all ways and always? And may the Spirit that was in Jesus dwell in our hearts and shine through our lives into the lives of countless others as we seek to live a truly "worthy," Christ-like life!

REV. EDWARD H. BONSALL, JR.,
Swarthmore, Pennsylvania.

"Who delivered us from so great a death, and doth deliver; in whom we trust that he will yet deliver us."
—2 Corinthians 1: 10.

THE apostle is speaking of physical deliverance. God had delivered him out of death when he had been in great peril. He was delivering him every day for he was never free from peril. He trusted that He would continue to deliver him until he would be called home.

We thus have an illustration of threefold spiritual deliverance of the believer in Jesus Christ. He is saved when he accepts Christ as Savior and Lord (Romans 10: 9, 10). He is in the process of salvation, growth in grace, thereafter through the indwelling of the Holy Spirit (Philippians 2: 12, 13). He is saved at last when his body is raised from the dead and glorified (Philippians 3: 20, 21).

REV. JAMES M. GRAY, D.D.,
Chicago, Illinois.

"Is it well with thee?"—2 Kings 4: 26.

SAY it and sing it jubilantly: "Is it well with my soul!" A triumphant spirit is trumpet testimony amidst all discouragements.

All is not "right with the world." Pray, therefore, and labor for the Kingdom of God:—the Spirit of Christ in every realm and relationship of life.

Test your character daily. Are you growing more Christ-like? Physical health is vital. Spiritual health is eternal and supreme.

With Christ as your Lord and Savior, "all's well that ends well." Blot out your past with the pardon of a boundless grace, face your present with the peace of an abiding trust, and go forward into your future with "the power of an endless life."

REV. CHARLES DANIEL BRODHEAD,
Jenkintown, Pennsylvania.

"What do ye more than others?"—Matthew 5: 47.

MANY people will never learn about the more abundant life from the Bible—they will not read it.

Many others will not discover Christian Truth at Church—they will not attend.

But we are open epistles to them—they read us like a book.

The chief hindrance to the coming of the Kingdom of Heaven on Earth is not the professing of Christianity but the practicing of Christianity. It is an axiom that, "Actions speak louder than words." When some people face such fact they are tempted to shorten their confession so as to meet the measurement of their actions. Such is contrary to the proposal of Jesus. He would not have us out-profess the professionals but He is eager that we out-do the ordinary.

REV. M. A. MARCY, D.D.,
Salem, Oregon.

"I am not ashamed of the gospel of Christ: for it is the power of God unto salvation to every one that believeth."— Romans 1: 16.

THE missionary rejoices in his *Gospel,* for he sees it transforming men and nations with a *Power* entirely supernatural. It brings the riches of Divine grace to body, mind and soul, potent alike with king and peasant, rich and poor, of whatever race or color or language. It seldom uproots people from their accustomed occupations, but takes them as they are and where they are— the plowman at his plow, the smith at his anvil, the merchant at his counter, the banker at his desk, the engineer at his throttle, the miner in his shaft, the seamstress at her needle, the stenographer at her keys, the mother at her cradle—and enobles the work as it sanctifies the worker. The Gospel is the transmission line of Divine Power.

REV. H. CARROLL WHITENER,
Albuquerque, New Mexico.

"Are not two sparrows sold for a farthing? and one of them shall not fall on the ground without your Father. But the very hairs of your head are all numbered."— Matthew 10: 29, 30.

JUST what is Jesus trying to say in these simple but beautiful words? Is it not that there is Some One in the universe Who is thinking of them, and Who cares for them and protects them?

He used every form of speech to try and make this blessed truth plain. He told them that nothing could happen to them however trivial or commonplace, that was not of interest to God. Look at that sparrow dead by the side of the road, how cheap a thing, and yet your Heavenly Father knows when a sparrow falls.

Somebody is thinking of you and caring for you, and if you trust Him, will bring you through, is what Jesus was telling the people of His day, and would tell us, too.

REV. HARRY H. BEATTYS,
Stamford, Connecticut.

"Fear not, Paul; thou must be brought before Cæsar, and lo, God hath given thee all them that sail with thee. Wherefore, sirs, be of good cheer; for I believe God, that it shall be even as it was told me."—Acts 27: 24, 25.

THE ship had been caught in a most terrific storm. For fourteen days and nights neither sun nor stars had appeared, and all hope that they should be saved was taken away.

St. Paul came on deck and stood in the midst of these terror-stricken seamen and passengers, and exclaimed "Sirs, be of good cheer." After hearing his message these men became calm and submissive, and turned over to this prisoner the sinking ship, and he gave them food to eat, and with the blessing of God upon them they were comforted.

With St. Paul now in charge of the ship, the man that God had trained, redeemed, owned, and used, the life of every man on board the ship was saved.

To know that we belong to God, that he has redeemed us, will inspire us to face the storms of life with courage and devotion, and with full assurance that He will use us in bringing about the fulfillment of His promise to us.

REV. GEORGE M. OAKLEY, D.D.,
Jenkintown, Pennsylvania.

"I am come that they might have life, and that they might have it more abundantly."—John 10: 10.

LIFE is sweet!" But, am I alive? Life is more than breathing, eating, playing, working. Life, in the Christian meaning, is purpose—Purpose with a capital 'P.' Remember how Silas Marner, losing his purpose, became little more than a lever of his loom. But, when little golden haired Eppie came into his heart he lived again. The abundance of Christ's life is revealed in the Cross. His love for us made Him willing to die for us. "Greater love hath no man than this, that a man lay down his life for his friends." The more one loves the more abundantly he lives. Love never fails. He alone can give it to us.

REV. LEROY S. EWING,
Pen Argyl, Pennsylvania.

"Then the same day at evening, being the first day of the week, when the doors were shut where the disciples were assembled for fear of the Jews, came Jesus and stood in the midst and saith unto them, Peace be unto you."— John 20: 19.

HERE is the eternal Miracle, the real presence of our living Lord in the midst of His disciples. They could bar the doors against the Jews, whom they feared, but not against Jesus, Whom they loved. Above all, it was His love that found the way in. Whatever the bolts and bars about our Souls, in reaching us, the self-confined prisoners of despair, "His love unknown, has broken every barrier down." Fear vanishes when Jesus comes into our lives. With the gift of peace, comes also the grace of pardon. "He showed unto them His hands and His side," those signs of His suffering and sacrifice for sinners on the Cross of Calvary. Then, revived by the indwelling Spirit, born anew, restored to gladness by the vision of the ever-present Christ, let us to our task of making disciples of all men.

REV. D. WALLACE CHRISTIE, B.D.,
Toronto, Ontario, Canada.

"For God so loved the world, that he gave his only be-gotten Son, that whosoever believeth in him should not perish, but have everlasting life."—John 3: 16.

IF COMPELLED to live with a single book, and but one verse of that book, I would say "give me the Bible, and write this verse of the Gospel on my heart"—"God so dearly loved this world that He freely *gave* His *only begotten son*—Upon His Cross." I read these emblazoned words, "Look unto me and be ye saved." The personal power, enabling me to see my Risen Lord, is The Holy Spirit, whose work is to show the things of Christ to the human soul—*"WHOSOEVER"*—means you, me and everybody—(Therefore "be-lieving" this precious promise, I can exultingly sing, "Glory be to the Father, and to the Son, and to the Holy Ghost; As it was in the beginning, is now and ever shall be, world without end.)

RT. REV. JAMES R. WINCHESTER, D.D.,
Memphis, Tennessee.

"Who comforteth us in all our tribulation, that we may be able to comfort them which are in any trouble, by the comfort wherewith we ourselves are comforted of God." 2 Corinthians 1: 4.

PAUL had much the same experience that we have. Nobody felt more than he the disappointments in life, the coldness and indifference around him, and yet he said, "I have learned in every state to be content." Perhaps the secret is found in our text. Good news helps us all; it inspires us to greater effort, so if we find the key to such an experience, that will indeed be good news. God comforts us by what He is, by what He does, by what He means to do. Oh, rest in God; things may change, friends may change, he never changes or fails. Just think for a moment the Shepherd of the stars is the Shepherd of His people. How near He comes in lowliness and sorrow. "The darkness brings out worlds of light we never saw by day." Remember the Creator, Preserver and Upholder of all things is your Comforter and Friend.

REV. FRANCIS E. PURCELL,
Middletown, Pennsylvania.

"So after he had washed their feet, and had taken his garments, and was set down again, he said unto them, Know ye what I have done to you?"—John 13: 12.

IN WASHING the feet of the disciples Jesus performed the task of a common slave, showing that no labor was too lowly if only it truly served. Some think that on this occasion the host had accidentally failed to provide the foot-washing slave; if so, Jesus met the emergency as He did at the wedding in Cana and through it taught the eternal lesson.

Serve or die is the law of nature. The useless are ultimately eliminated in human as well as animal life. Eventually genuine service surmounts prejudice and opposition. Jesus is thus conquering the world. No other teacher of religion has so served the race nor upheld the ideal of service. He thus fulfills the prophet's vision, "Behold My servant Whom I have chosen." Absolute commitment to a life of service is the test of discipleship.

REV. W. WOFFORD T. DUNCAN, D.D., LL.D.,
Pittsburgh, Pennsylvania.

"What hast thou that thou didst not receive?"—1 Corinthians 4: 7.

ALL that we are and all that we have we owe to God. We are so prone to forget all His benefits! In the favors and mercies He bestows, we should see the beating heart of Infinite Love. The Lord gives to us that we may help others. Since He has no needs for Himself, He expects us to use His portion to care for the needy, in body and soul, near at home, and to provide for the needier still, in all the earth, who perish for want of the Bread of Life. A Christian who gives in this spirit and from this motive has the promise of the life that now is, and of that which is to come. In the presence of the many blessings of God, we may well confess, "All things come of Thee, and of Thine own have we given Thee."

REV. ALLEN R. BARTHOLOMEW, D.D., D.T., LL.D.,
Philadelphia, Pennsylvania.

"For we are His workmanship, created in Christ Jesus."
—Ephesians 2: 10.

WORKMANSHIP" in the Greek is "Poiema," our English "poem." It also means "Masterpiece." All who believe in the Lord Jesus Christ and accept Him as the only Savior, find in Him redemption and receive eternal life. They are a new creation. He takes such as we are, by nature dead in sins and enemies, and gives us His life. He bestows upon us His Spirit and we become His children, forgiven and accepted in the Beloved One. Ultimately all the redeemed will be transformed into His image and share His inheritance in glory. "We shall be like Him, for we shall see Him as He is." This glorious redemption is God's Masterpiece, the beautiful poem of His Love and Grace.

Rev. ARNO C. GAEBELEIN, D.D.,
New York, New York.

"Father, forgive them; for they know not what they do."
—Luke 23: 34.

CALVARY is the watershed of world events! At once it is the darkest, most awful and most illuminating scene of all ages, filled with unfathomable depths and infinite, majestic heights. How shall we interpret the meaning of it all?

The representative throng about the Cross can bring us no light. The Sanhedrin and the soldiers were blind and unmoved. The friends and followers were overwhelmed with sorrow and there was no light upon that Cross for them. Where, then, shall we find Calvary in its true light?

It is in the mind of Christ Himself that we see the clear meaning of it all. Out of the gathering mists of death He spoke those words which are as windows of His mind; fragments only, but charged with eternal significance and stamped with the image of Himself.

Of tremendous significance is the fact that He first prayed. His public ministry opened with prayer. Now it was closing with prayer. "Father, forgive them, they know not what they do."

REV. STEWART P. MACLENNAN, D.D.,
Hollywood, California.

"I would know him in the power of his resurrection and the fellowship of his sufferings, with my nature transformed to die as he died, to see if I too can attain the resurrection from the dead. ... I press forward to appropriate it, because I have been appropriated myself by Christ Jesus."—Philippians 3: 10–12. Moffatt's Translation.

THE peak of Jesus' ministry is the cross because in this experience he taught mankind the sublimity of suffering. Without the cross there could have been no resurrection, and without the resurrection the ongoing spiritual life would have no foundation.

The apostle Paul is expressing a desire in this passage to identify himself completely with the Christ. His message speaks of the vital elements in Christianity. Power, fellowship, transformation, and attainment all come through the one channel of fellowship with the living Christ.

This fellowship goes to the very depths of religious experience and lives completely in the atmosphere of Christly thinking. In this spirit the true Christian goes forward to appropriate eternal life because he has been appropriated by Christ Jesus.

REV. CHARLES EDGAR CATHEY,
Batesville, Mississippi.

"So teach us to number our days, that we may apply our hearts unto wisdom. . . . O satisfy us early with thy mercy; that we may rejoice and be glad all our days. . . . Let thy work appear unto thy servants."—Psalms 90: 12–16.

THE 90th Psalm has been called the dirge of humanity. Tradition has attributed it to Moses and certainly there could be no more fitting background for its august periods of ruin than the Wilderness wandering, with its toll of a whole generation.

But Moses, tearing loose from what must have seemed to him the dark and dreadful shapes of universal night, lays hold upon the everlasting God and cries out for wisdom, gladness and a vision of the on-going purposes of the Eternal.

May we get from it all, O God, a heart of wisdom. Transmute it all for us with the unspeakable joy of Thy presence, like sunrise in a tomb. And grant us a vision of the armies still sweeping through the gates. The workers fall, but the work goes on. Sink our mortality in the immortality of thy marching plans.

REV. HENRY M. EDMONDS,
Birmingham, Alabama.

"And he entered into one of the ships, which was Simon's,
. . . and he sat down and taught the people."—Luke 5 : 3.

THE men were discouraged. They had toiled
all night and had caught nothing, and their
living depended on the success of their work.
Then Jesus appeared and did a very strange thing.
He asked them to help Him with the very thing
they had been using, the boat in which they had
been such a failure.

Into our discouraged lives Jesus comes with a
similar request. He asks for our coöperation.
If we grant His request our feeling of uselessness
will leave us, and our discouragement will dis-
appear, for we will always remember that Jesus
wanted us, and could use what we had to speak
to people who might never have heard Him without our help.

It is a wonderful thing that He asks for just
what we have, the thing to which we have grown
accustomed, and think of little value, our boat.

REV. G. S. BECKWITH,
Providence, Rhode Island.

"Hast thou not known? hast thou not heard, that the everlasting God, the Lord, the Creator of the ends of the earth, fainteth not, neither is weary? there is no searching of his understanding."—Isaiah 40: 28.

THE thought of a God Who does not weary is the antidote for human despondency. We are not adequate to the tasks which confront us, but how sublimely He is adequate, in wisdom, in strength, and in love! His life is universal, and pervades the universe which He has created. The telescope brings us word of His power from galaxies of stars whose far flashings take a million light-years to reach us; the microscope reveals His laws of beauty in underseas formations of fairylike delicacy and perfection of form. If we can but wait upon this Lord of nature and of grace and center our thought in this profound center of all thought and of life, then strength comes back to us, and refreshment, and a springtide of renewal.

REV. HOWARD CHANDLER ROBBINS, D.D.,
New York City, New York.

"Abide in me, and I in you."—John 15:4.

JESUS was, and is, God's life extension plan for the whole of humanity. The best Bible binding is human flesh. Personality is the essential vehicle in the divine procedure for the perpetuation of the spiritual life.

Christ within! What is He there for? To inspire confidence in Himself and all that is righteous; to inspire hope, without which, even the living are dead; to inspire vision—visions of God in the highest and at the fingertips of men. He is there, also, to warn us of the dangers that hurt. Whatever hurts us hurts Him.

What a joy, Christ within! Checking the evil and calling out the good; Christ within; evil habits, bad tastes, hatreds without. Pray that He may be born in many hearts today.

REV. J. OSBUN PHILLIPS,
Butte, Montana.

"Eye hath not seen, nor ear heard, neither have entered into the heart of man, the things which God hath prepared for them that love Him."—1 Corinthians 2: 9.

I T IS natural for Christians to think much on the future home of endless years. Yet in our fondest imaginings, we can picture but a woefully inadequate heaven. Our idea is formed from our little earthly mediocrities, the places and things our eyes have seen, the sounds and words our ears have heard, the desires and ecstasies of our human hearts. Just as a lowly creature of the deep and lightless sea could not know the world above, a world of sunshine and air and human complexities, so we, geared to the dust, can not know "things which God hath prepared for them that love Him."

God is always better than our most daring hopes of Him. Heaven will be, for all who enter there, an Utmost Surprise.

REV. WILLIAM M. ERHARD,
Clarksburg, West Virginia.

"Jesus . . . lifted up his eyes to heaven, and said, Father . . ."—John 17: 1.

JESUS sometimes prayed with His eyes wide open. He does so on this occasion. He faces the cross looking straight into the eyes of God. No other attitude could suffice. The clear, clean passion of His soul reaches up into the clear, full light of His Father's will and love, and craves companionship.

Nor does he close His eyes upon His brother's world thereby, but lifts it in clearer vision while He prays, to the waiting heart of love.

So would I face my world each day; with eyes so clear and clean that every look may bring me nearer God and other men; remembering that to be a Christian there must be three: God, myself, and my brother.

REV. PERLEY C. GRANT, D.D.,
Barre, Vermont.

"For their sakes I sanctify myself."—John 17: 19.

THESE are the noblest words ever uttered by man. To try to save one's own soul only is selfish and so clean contrary to the heart of Christianity. But to make one's self holy for the sake of others is unselfish and also the highest type of service. Character is the world's greatest need, and character, good or bad, is contagious. In proportion as I make myself stronger, braver, kinder, truer, purer, I am adding to the sum total of goodness in the world and so making it easier for others to do right. This is the paradox of unselfish selfishness, of interest in self, not merely for one's own good but for the sake of others. We rightly think often of the holiness of service but not enough of the service of holiness.

RT. REV. G. ASHTON OLDHAM, D.D., S.T.D.,
Albany, New York.

"My help cometh from the Lord, which made heaven and earth. . . . He that keepeth thee will not slumber."—Psalms 121: 2, 3.

GOD was our help in ages past, our hope for ages to come. He grants us this day an uplifting consciousness of His presence.

We offer unto Him the gratitude of our hearts for the life which He has given, for the beauty of the world, for the daily task in which we are able to forget ourselves and minister unto others, for our loved ones, for health, food, clothing, shelter, and sunshine. Out of the depth of our hearts we thank Him for forgiveness of sins and the assurance of approval.

He has given us the night to rest from our labors, and as we start on the new day, gives us grace to begin and courage to pursue our task. We ask His guidance to help us to achieve victories and to shun evil.

REV. EDWARD FORREST,
Waldron, Arkansas.

"Behold, now is the accepted time; behold, now is the day of salvation."—2 Corinthians 6: 2.

CLEARLY the emphatic word of life, as also in this verse, is the word "Now." For who can tell of tomorrow? God here challenges us with deciding definitely for Him today; completely, wholly, surrendering.

What need for haste? Much! With the rising of the sun, tomorrow shall become today; with the setting thereof, today shall fade into yesterday. It is the All-Knowing One Who warns us that now it is high time for us to wake out of sleep.

Behold, my little children, now is the acceptable time. Today the Father's offer of grace, forgiveness, and reconciliation is extended to us. Let our souls be roused, and our wills be stirred to rise up in His might, and lay hold of that offer this day. It shall become our day of salvation.

REV. DANIEL D. KISTLER,
Everett, Washington.

As the hart panteth after the water brooks,
So panteth my soul after thee, O God.
My soul thirsteth for God, for the living God.
                    —Psalm 42: 1, 2.

WHY does the human heart cry out for God, finding no enduring satisfaction except in Him?

A vital experience of God furnishes the outlook upon life which makes for abundant and fruitful living, which, extending beyond the individual, includes within its radius of vision and appreciation other groups, other classes, other nations. It inspires ever-challenging, ever-impelling ideals and standards rising above the petty self-interests of individuals and groups. It constitutes an irresistible dynamic, holding men steady in the hour of temptation, struggle and disillusionment, and impelling them toward the ultimate realization of their ideals. It is an unfailing source of comfort and consolation in the hour of sorrow and bereavement, of renewing inspiration in the presence of moral and spiritual failure, tragedy and defeat.

REV. FREDERICK CARL EISELEN, PH.D., D.D., LL.D.,
    Evanston, Illinois.

"But ye shall receive power, after that the Holy Ghost is come upon you: and ye shall be witnesses unto me both in Jerusalem, and in all Judea, and in Samaria, and unto the uttermost part of the earth."—Acts 1: 8.

GOD the Holy Ghost is more sinned against than any of the three persons in the Holy Trinity. Because, He is abiding here now and yet we do not recognize Him. God is not here, as He was in the days of His flesh. He is now at the right hand of the Father as our Advocate. But Jesus said: "I will send to you the Holy Ghost as He will abide with you for ever." Jesus also said: "Ye shall receive power after that the Holy Ghost is come upon you."

The Holy Ghost came upon Peter with power at Pentecost. After that Peter's preaching and practicing was in the Power of the Spirit. This same power is available for each one who reads this. You, perhaps, are resisting that Power and grieving that Spirit. But He is waiting to clothe you with supernatural power, that you may go from victory to victory.

REV. JOHN GIBSON INKSTER, D.D.,
Toronto, Ontario, Canada.

"My grace is sufficient for thee."——2 Corinthians 12 : 9.

IT WOULD have been comforting to know that God's grace had been historically sufficient, or will be at some future date. But an ever-present sufficiency is imperative for my life's needs each moment.

Because this promise is in the present-tense, it enters my consciousness with challenging, reviving, strengthening power in the hours when I am disappointed, discouraged, disillusioned, prosperous, prayerless, pleasure-bent, suffering, sorrowing, straying, weary in body, mind or soul.

The only time His grace seems insufficient is when I forget or neglect to utilize that grace.

In your every hour of need, test this promise with an active, vital faith and you too will find His grace sufficient for thee!

REV. JOHN N. LINK, S.T.D.,
Baltimore, Maryland.

"And hath given to us the ministry of reconciliation."—
2 Corinthians 5 : 18.

THE supreme responsibility of the Disciples of
Jesus is the task of reconciliation. The imperative emphasis in this ministry is within the
antagonisms of human life. Most of our antagonisms root in the rich and varied endowments of
human nature and are, therefore, the tokens of
our greatness· and not of our littleness. Antagonisms arise not because one side is entirely right
and the other entirely wrong, but because there is
a right on both sides for which it is worthwhile to
contend and a wrong on both sides by which our
vision of the other right is obscured.

Our problem is not to destroy antagonisms but
to transcend and transform them. It is possible
to get below, rise above, or pass through them into
a higher, nobler unity. The path to reconciliation lies within the temper of mind, the quality
of spirit seen in Jesus. The social value in any
man's life depends upon spiritual quality; not
on what he possesses, not upon what he knows but
upon what he is in the spirit of his life.

REV. RAYMOND C. BROOKS,
Claremont, California.

"And we know that all things work together for good to them that love God."—Romans 8:28.

EVERY person has protracted conflicts with self, Satan, the world, adversity, and sorrow; and is often left discouraged. At such a time as this we need the message of invigorating truth. It changes the aspect of every conflict of life. Trials of life are not to injure us, but to benefit; not to bring loss, but gain; we shall not be defeated, but conquer. Such a conviction inspires courage, kindles enthusiasm, and adorns us with strength. However, the promise is only to such that love God, and obedience is the infallible test of this love.

There is a distinction between those that love God and those that do not, because if all things worked together for good to all, good and bad alike, God would be sanctioning sin. God loves His own eternal purposes of truth and righteousness, and He most especially loves those who are fulfilling those purposes. It is a blessed relationship to love God and to be loved by Him.

REV. KIRBY M. YIENGST,
Maytown, Pennsylvania.

"Oh that I might have my request; and that God would grant me the thing that I long for!"—Job 6: 8.

JOB breathes the desire of every believer. We have faith but we do not see why the affliction comes, why the answer to prayer does not come. Yet the only real prayer our lips can utter will be the prayer for the will of God to be made manifest in our lives. When we ask in sincerity that His will be done, He will answer. The passion of the Son of God from His Barmitzvah in the temple as a boy of twelve till Heaven turned its face from the darkness of Golgotha was the will of God. To be in His blessed will means to be in the current of Divine Blessing. The answer may be fire, smoke and blood. "He knows and lives and cares, nothing this truth can dim. He gives the very best to those who leave the choice with Him." Paul asked for the removal of the thorn but was content with the sufficiency of His grace. The Apostle's strength was made perfect in weakness.

REV. RUSSELL TAYLOR SMITH, M.A., B.D.,
Philadelphia, Pennsylvania.

"Lead me to the rock that is higher than I."—Psalm 61: 2.

LAST summer a party of us lost our way among the lakes of Ontario. A violent storm came up, but we found shelter under a great rock till the storm raged past. Then we resumed our hunt dispiritedly, until one said, "Let us climb this rock; we may spy the trail from the top." It was a hard climb, but the challenge of the rock restored our courage. As we conquered the heights we gained confidence and mastery, and the hill-top gave us a vision of the way out.

Let that be a homely parable for us in the presence of "the Rock of our salvation." We long for protection. The Psalmist's prayer is often ours—but just for protection? The call of our Master is to courage and daring. The very loftiness of His life and character is a challenge to "rise on stepping-stones of our dead selves to higher things." Christ sets no limit to the height of our achievement in Himself. Then at the top there is the vista, our way clear in view. There, like Moses, we may see God "face to face."

REV. JULIUS F. SEEBACH,
Philadelphia, Pennsylvania

"A man's gift maketh room for him."—Proverbs 18: 16.

WE MAY this day lift life's horizon. The outpouring of beautiful helpful service, in whatever form it may take, makes room for one in the heart of another. Our gifts may not be of money, but of thoughtful deeds, kind words, a sympathetic smile.

Likewise, a man's own heart is kept pure and wholesome and sweet by the outpouring of service, whatever form it may take.

We make room for ourselves in the heart of God in the same way. "Come, ye blessed of my Father, inherit the kingdom prepared for you . . . for I was an hungered, and ye gave me meat . . . inasmuch as ye did it unto one of the least of these my brethren, ye did it unto me."

REV. EZRA ALLEN VAN NUYS,
San Francisco, California.

"In this was manifested the love of God toward us, because that God sent his only begotten Son into the world, that we might live through him."—1 John 4: 9.

A FATHER has many ways of expressing his love for his child and the heavenly Father has very many more ways. Man looks up into the heavens and sees the stars as messengers of God's love. Man turns to the violets at his feet and hears them telling the story of God's love. But the greatest expression of God's love is the entrance of the Divine Son into our life to share our experiences, aid in our conflicts, help in our daily work, and lead the way into the unknown world. Love could go no farther. Love needed to go no farther. With love divine came life abundant and eternal. God shared everything with His children. Let us accept his love gratefully and lovingly and live obediently and expectantly.

REV. HARRY GLENN FINNEY, D.D.,
Fayetteville, Arkansas.

"So teach us to number our days, that we may apply our hearts unto wisdom."—Psalm 90: 12.

HOW the emphasis rests upon the *day* as the natural unit of time in human experience! Every day is a fresh beginning: "Swift to its close ebbs out life's little day!" The Shepherd Psalm leads us from morning to evening. The Lord's Prayer teaches us to say:—Give us our bread; forgive us our debts; deliver us from evil, —day by day. Thus then let us plan our lives.

May each day begin and close in fellowship with our heavenly Father *through prayer;* including a period of pause to hear what He shall say to us. May the common toil of each day bear evidence that the increase of God's kingdom is the highest aim of our daily service. May each day be enriched by *sacrificial giving,* so that we may learn to lay up our treasure in heaven.

By a daily plan such as this "May we apply our hearts unto wisdom."

REV. J. RAUCH STEIN, D.D.,
Philadelphia, Pennsylvania.

"And the Lord smelled a sweet savour."—Genesis 8: 21.

YOU have your favorite perfume. It may be heliotrope or attar of roses or lily of the valley. How sweet to your smell is the delicate scent of the violet! Just so God has His favorite perfume. Nothing is so sweet to Him as the sincere, grateful worship of His Children. Noah's sacrifice was the expression of his grateful trust in God. Have we any cause for praise? Let our thanksgivings rise like sweet incense. "His name, like sweet perfume, shall rise with every morning sacrifice." Let us bring to our family altar our sincere thanksgivings, trusting for acceptance in Him who "hath loved us and hath given Himself for us an offering and a sacrifice to God for a sweet smelling savor."

REV. IRVING MAXWELL,
Camden, New Jersey.

"Blessed is the Man."—Psalm 1:1.

PERHAPS our nearest approach to the psalmist's meaning would be to say, "O, the blessednesses of the man."

This is not mere happiness. Happiness is rooted in "hap" and depends on what happens. If the right thing happens you are happy. If the wrong thing, you are unhappy.

Happiness is an emotion. Blessedness is a condition. The drunkard might be happy wallowing in the mire but he wouldn't be blessed.

Happiness is like the mercury in the thermometer going up and down with the weather. Blessedness is like the life of the palm tree ignoring the dry sand and striking its root down to concealed waters. Blessedness is a state above circumstances.

There was a strange character who frequently in the prayer meeting said, "I feel as good when I don't feel good as I do when I do feel good."

O, the blessedness of the New Birth; relationship to the Father; fellowship with Christ and an inheritance waiting!

REV. WILL H. HOUGHTON,
New York, New York.

"Let not your heart be troubled: ye believe in God, believe also in me."—John, 14: 1.

FAITH is a fact, as much a fact as life and death are facts. In all human history man has believed and, believing, has claimed a future existence. To call this anticipation of a conscious state beyond the grave a mere superstition, a figment of desire, a bright phantasy conjured to set over against the dark phantom of fear, is not enough. There is an inevitability about immortality. It is the logical conclusion of a man's thought concerning himself.

Today we have a mysterious yet vitalizing assurance that we are not outward bound, but homeward bound. And so, though at times the seas be rough and the winds high, we look through windows of pain and disaster, upon the rising shore lines of the coast of deliverance, the continent of reunion, the land of fulfilment!

REV. DANIEL A. POLING, D.D., LL.D.,
Boston, Massachusetts.

"But the angel of the Lord by night opened the prison doors, and brought them forth, and said, Go, stand and speak in the temple to the people all the words of this life."— Acts 5: 19, 20.

MEN are to be saved by Christianity and we must feel the responsibility to give the message, for it is still true that men are saved "by the words of this life." The world has tried various nostrums and opiates which have failed. We must give the vision of the Christ for the American trails of life.

Every man's religion and salvation is his own personal affair. We give another man light but it is his inevitable responsibility to act upon the light.

Big, human and spiritual interests are institutionalized. It is our duty to make the institution of home life Christian in standards, affection, and unity. If our home life is a failure we can easily understand the cause of the youth problems of our day. It is our duty to give home life Christian atmosphere and tone.

It is our duty to feel church responsibility. The state of the church today elicits various comments but the biggest factor in the decline of spiritual power is the failure in our duty to our church. All our gifts should be consecrated to the service of the church.

REV. FRANK M. SILSLEY, D.D.,
Evanston, Illinois.

"He saved others; himself he cannot save."—Mark 15: 31.

HOW literally true are the words of this text, though spoken by sinful lips in scorn and derision! Jesus could not save Himself from the Cross, and at the same time save others. He chose to save others. For this choice He sweat drops of blood in Gethsemane, and for it He died on Calvary. Even in His dying hour He thought of others, making a home for His mother, praying for His enemies, and saving a thief from sin. And now that He has saved me from sin, I pray for daily grace to serve Him, by helping others.

"Others Lord, yes, others,"
Let this my motto be.
Help me to live for others
That I might live like Thee.

REV. W. F. BRADLEY, D.D.,
Carthage, Missouri.

"They that wait upon the Lord shall renew their strength."—Isaiah 40:31.

TO BE strong is a passion with most people. This touch of nature makes us all kin. Old and young, wise and ignorant, all of us thrill to the inner urge after strength. We long to be vigorous and capable, physically, mentally or spiritually. Certainly, we have a hankering after one of these; maybe after two, or even after all three.

Our age is coming to see that the profoundest possibilities in the attainment of strength go deeper than muscular development. A mind at peace and a soul undistressed are vital to the largest and longest attainment of all round strength. We come to the fulfillment of our largest capabilities when we are at-one-ment with the heart of the universe, with the power that made us.

REV. WILLIAM E. HAMMAKER, D.D., LL.D., *Youngstown, Ohio.*

"There is, therefore, now no condemnation to them which are in Jesus Christ."—Romans 8: 1.

THESE words imply that there is a condemnation for those who are not in Christ. By sin men have deserved condemnation, and there is no escape except through Christ the Savior. *Secondly,* the believers are in Christ, and are surrounded, protected and shielded by Him. They are safe so long as they are in Christ. *Thirdly,* there is no condemnation for those who believe in Christ. St. Paul does not say maybe, or perhaps, or I hope that there is no condemnation, but he says positively there is no condemnation for them that are in Christ Jesus. The believer should have no doubt on this point. His forgiveness and salvation for Christ's sake are sure.

REV. JOSEPH STUMP, D.D., LL.D., L.H.D.,
Minneapolis, Minnesota.

"As thy days, so shall thy strength be."—Deuteronomy 33: 25.

THE world is full of changes. Old things are being swept away. Old landmarks have been left behind. What a comfort to turn our minds to the triumphant certainties that have not changed. It was in such an age as our own that a great prophetic soul committed to a thinking, groping world the priceless message: "As thy days, so shall thy strength be." Whatever tomorrow may bring of joy or of sorrow, of bane or of blessing, with the coming of the burden, we have God's promises of strength.

This priceless passage is not only a promise, it is a record of the life experience of millions of believers. Just such an experience led the great shepherd king, after one of the darkest experiences of his career, to give expression to that glorious psalm, "The Lord is my Shepherd, I shall not want. Though I walk through the valley of the shadow of death I shall fear no evil for Thou art with me."

May this battle cry of a pilgrim soul become a personal experience to all of us.

REV. HENRY W. A. HANSON, D.D., LL.D.,
Gettysburg, Pennsylvania.

"If any man have not the Spirit of Christ, he is none of his."—Romans 8:9.

IT IS one thing to possess the world of Jesus, but quite another thing to possess the spirit of Christ. If only we who profess His name and wear the badge of His Church in the rough and tumble of this life, possessed in our hearts, and manifested in all our human relations the Spirit of Christ, what vitality it would impart to the whole Christian enterprise, and how it would lift the moral level of society.

Don't ask me to define the Spirit of Christ. It eludes definition, though it is as clear to you as your mother's love, and Paul's statement is crystal clear, like an axiom in mathematics.

The message of this verse goes straight to the heart of all of us. "If any man have not the Spirit of Christ, he is none of his."

REV. ALBERT JOSEPH McCARTNEY,
Washington, D. C.

"God breathed into his nostrils the breath of life; and man became a living soul."—Genesis 2: 7.

THE Spirit of God has always sought, since man existed, to breathe into the spirit of man . . . into all men, not only a chosen people, a chosen church. The Spirit of God is as much occupied with the hearts of men in the gambling den, or the drunken dive at this moment, as with the heart of a saint. Everywhere, in every race, in every place, in every individual, the Spirit of God is at work.

If we open our beings to the Spirit of God, he will conduct us into the hard and happy School of Development. He will lead us through the Halls of Spiritual Learning. Without change and growth the pulse of life beats feebly.

REV. ROBERT JOHNSTON, D.D.,
Washington, D. C.

"For unto you is born this day, in the city of David, a Savior, which is Christ the Lord."—Luke 2: 11.

EVERY Christmas is but another rainbow flashing the promise, "God with us," to the world. May our hearts be attuned to the Angelic Chorus, "Glory to God, etc." This is the message of God's love for humanity. His love has created a mighty camp in every land that is guarded by obedient hands. There are some in every nation, that kneeling, hail Him with newborn spirit. Messages of good will are flashed and written—the great universe jubilates, and as the genial warmth of this joy is suffused to our hearts may we be moved at this time, above all others, make glad with Christmas joy, the hearts of those whom God has placed along our way.

May Thy love constrain us to serve Thee, Gracious Savior.

REV. BENJAMIN A. SAND,
Vancouver, British Columbia, Canada.

"And she brought forth her firstborn son, and wrapped him in swaddling clothes, and laid him in a manger, because there was no room for them in the inn."—Luke 2: 7.

CAN you put yourself in the place of an adult who is reading for the first time the wonderful story of the birth of Jesus? Missionaries have the delightful experience of listening to the comments of some of those to whom the story comes thus in absolute freshness, and they tell of the amazement of these people who have lived in heathenism. The idea that the Son of God should be born like any other babe! And to think that there was no room for him! Let these thoughts sink into the heart as if they had never been heard before. Thoughtful dwelling on them must awaken new love and adoration for Jesus, and stronger determination that always there shall be room for Him in the temple of the living God of which we hold the key.

REV. JOHN T. FARIS, D.D.,
Philadelphia, Pennsylvania.

"Wist ye not that I must be in my Father's house!"
—Luke 2: 49. Revised Version.

WHEN the parents of the boy Jesus, after anxiously seeking, found Him in the Temple, He said to His mother, "Did you not know that I must be active in my Father's affairs?"

There was a great urge in the heart of Jesus, unknown even to His mother. Every Christian life should feel the compulsion of a purpose. When the appeal of reason and faith desert us, we must depend upon the "I must."

Good purposes, high ideals, Christian faith— life's greatest achievements are not always to be pursued because of pleasure and allurement. They have their dead spots of discouragement and temptation. When the fog obscures the true perspective of life, when fatigue threatens our vitality, the compulsion of "I must" may furnish the additional necessary push over the goal.

For the sake of others, for the sake of right, yes above all for the sake of my Lord, "I must" be Christian in my faith, in my service.

REV. CALVIN P. SWANK, D.D.
Philadelphia, Pennsylvania.

"I have set the Lord always before me."—Psalm 16: 8.

THE writer of the song has realized the divine presence. The unique part of his experience is the fact that it is not momentary and evanescent. It is abiding. He has discovered the only safe ground to make proper judgment. He is in reality a disciple in the higher school of the Spirit. What a difference it will make in our behavior if we will realize this attitude for just one day. The secret places from whence come the issues of life can now only send forth pure motives; our words shall be chosen with utmost care; selfish and mean thoughts will be slain in their infancy. Such a one will realize increasingly the privilege of discipleship. He lives only to do the will of God. In St. Paul's phraseology, "For me to live is Christ."

REV. E. CLYDE XANDER,
Greenville, Pennsylvania.

"He would grant . . . that ye may be strengthened with power through his Spirit in the inward man; that Christ may dwell in your hearts through faith; to the end that ye, being rooted and grounded in love, may be strong to apprehend with all the saints what is the breadth and length and height and depth, and to know the love of Christ which passeth knowledge, that ye may be filled unto all the fullness of God."—Ephesians 3: 16–19. Revised Version.

A BOLD prayer! Its boldness based on the conviction of the limitless riches of divine glory. Addressed to the Father of all men. The prayer of one who knew and met the conditions of effective praying—Humility, reverence, earnestness and faith.

The world needs men strong of heart today, with this power which comes through the Spirit. Each of us needs and may have blessed fellowship if Christ makes his home in our hearts. No knowledge is comparable to that which is of his love. The fullness of God with all his holiness may be in us. Thus will our spiritual life be deepened as Paul prayed that it might be long years ago.

REV. WILLIAM CLAUDE WALTEMYER, PH.D.,
Gettysburg, Pennsylvania.

"There is, therefore, now no condemnation to them which are in Christ Jesus, who walk not after the flesh, but after the Spirit."—Romans 8: 1.

BLESSED assurance. No condemnation in conscience, in memory, in sin. Free! Free from the law, from sin, from death and its penalty.

How cluttered life becomes with the multitude of wearying, depressing, defeating worries and concerns. How utterly impotent is the heart and will of man to free him from this terrific and appalling bondage of the flesh. But what man cannot do God has done. "Sending His own Son in the likeness of sinful flesh, He has condemned sin in the flesh." And now in Him life has become changed. Our troubles, sorrows, burdens, weaknesses, all take on radiant significance in the light of His Cross.

We were weak but in Him we are made strong. We were empty but in Him we are filled. We were hungry but in Him we are fed. Now life becomes vital, meaningful, radiant with possibilities for happiness. We are blessed, forgiven, saved. "Thanks be to God who gaveth us the victory through our Lord Jesus Christ."

REV. J. LOWREY FENDRICH, D.D.,
Brooklyn, New York.

"And the street of the city was pure gold."—Revelation 21: 21.

AT LAST gold has found its place. It is a thing to stand on, to walk on, to make progress over, not to be crowned with. The new order obtains. The last is become the first. The new life begins where the old did end. The last and best of earthly desire is the initial step of heavenly activity. The vague hypotheses of Time are the postulates of Eternity. We stand "on what too long we bore with shoulders bent and downcast eyes," and, standing, behold a new cosmology. Surely heaven's estimate must be the right one. Precious stones must belong in the foundation of the City's walls, and precious metal in the paving blocks of her street. They are servants, and have no place in the edifice of character save as they serve.

REV. ROBERT FREEMAN, D.D., LITT.D., *Pasadena, California.*